Our Lady

Norman Pittenger

Our Lady

The Mother of Jesus in Christian Faith
and Devotion

SCM PRESS LTD

0 334 02627 X

First Published 1996
by SCM Press Ltd
9–17 St Albans Place, London N1 0NX

Printed and bound in Great Britain by
Biddles Ltd, Guildford and King's Lynn

For
Nigel Hancock

friend through many years

Contents

Preface

This is my last book; and for reasons which will appear later in this preface it seems to me right that its subject should be St Mary, the Mother of Jesus, often called in Catholic Christian devotion 'Our Lady'. But not only is this my last book; it is my ninetieth published book. My first book was *The Approach to Christianity*, published in 1939 by the long-since vanished Centenary Press in London. Most of the copies of that book were destroyed later that year in the bombing of London by the Nazis; it was again brought out (three years later) by Cloister Press in the United States in an American edition under the title of *The Christian Way in the Modern World*; and in 1952, once more in Britain, SCM Press published it as *Principles and Practice of Christian Faith*.

These ninety books have dealt with a considerable variety of topics. Most of them, whether published in Britain or in the United States, have been concerned with Christian theology. Some have discussed questions in Christian ethics, sacramental life and worship, and aspects of Christian discipleship. Nine have been 'historical', among them a number of biographies in a series of books appearing from Franklin Watts of New York in the 1960s and early 70s, under the general head 'Immortals of History'. Besides all these books I have written many essays on religious topics as well as dozens of book reviews. All this writing has been done while I have been busily engaged in lecturing and teaching, first at the General Theological Seminary in New York and then here in Cambridge.

I have written the above summary, not to boast of my

productivity, but to indicate that during a long life, now reaching its early nineties, I have been actively concerned to look at many aspects of life within the ongoing Christian tradition; but hitherto I have not written anything specifically about St Mary save for one essay (which appeared in *The Anglican Theological Review* in 1951) on 'The Place of St Mary in Catholic Devotion'. Yet from my early days in my own personal religious life I have entertained for her a considerable devotion. For I was brought up in the variety of Anglican Christianity which by many used to be styled 'High Church' but which we who 'belonged' called Anglo-Catholicism. Whatever may have been my vagaries theologically, I have always been, and I remain, on the 'Catholic' side of things. Therefore it seems right that my theological career be brought to its end by a book on St Mary, 'Our Lady', and her important place in the broad Catholic Christian tradition.

I begin with historical matters: what do we 'know' about St Mary and how do we know it (if that is the proper way of phrasing it)? I proceed to see her as 'the consenting cause' (the phrase used in the Middle Ages) for what God accomplished in the event of Jesus Christ. I then consider her as a 'model' for Christian discipleship, as a 'type' of the church and a symbol of the world 'redeemed by God'. There follows a discussion of the devotion given her during the centuries of Christian history. And the book concludes with comments on 'the practical value' of 'mariological' devotion and an indication of what that devotion can contribute to the Christian faith in God.

I do not assume that what is here presented will meet with anything like general approval. Conservative Christians will probably think that in many respects I am far too sceptical about supposedly historical data. Liberally-minded persons, and not least those who like me accept the wider conceptuality known as 'Process Thought', will probably say that what I have written has been due to a nostalgic concern to maintain, somehow or other, what as a young boy and in my early manhood I was taught as 'the faith'. 'Catholics' may think that I have not said enough or that I have said it inadequately; 'Protestants' may regard the whole exercise as absurd and unbiblical, at best an irrelevance and at worst a superstitious addendum which damages the 'purity of the gospel'. I am aware of these possible attitudes; yet I am convinced that what is said in this book has importance and value. Therefore, for what it is worth, I send it out in the hope that it may be of interest to those who appreciate the beauty and richness of mariological devotion but yet are very conscious of new circumstances, new knowledge and new conditions presented by the contemporary world.

I must express my deep gratitude to those who much more than seventy or eighty years ago first instructed me in the Catholic 'way' of being a Christian. I am indebted also to many good friends, like the one to whom I have dedicated this book, who like me wish to retain and use whatever is of abiding value in this part of our inherited tradition but who do not for a moment deny their knowledge of the contemporary world, the results of the study of Christian origins, and the necessary re-conception of the tradition in our modern situation. For the way in which I have gone about the task and for whatever is said in these pages, of course I alone am responsible.

Since this is to be my last published book, I have ventured to ask my publisher to include, at the end of this volume, a list of my earlier books. I do this because a number of people have requested just such a list; and I hope that it does not seem immodest thus to respond to their request. Copies of all these books (and of everything else published by me) are deposited at the library of the General Seminary, 175 Ninth Avenue, New York, NY, USA, whose then librarian, Dr Nils Sonné asked for this material when I left New York and came to Cambridge in England.

1

History and Myth

The Abbé Alfred Loisy, one of the French leaders of the Roman Catholic Modernist Movement from 1890 to 1910 and a brilliant if sceptical biblical scholar, once wrote that about St Mary, mother of Jesus, we know *rien de rien* – 'nothing at all'.

That was an exaggerated statement. In the New Testament there are a considerable number of references to Mary – although, to be sure, none of them can be accepted as indubitable historical fact. What we know about her is found in material which must be studied and interpreted in accordance with the scholarly criteria that we use when engaging in any enquiry of this sort; but we expect scholars not to dismiss all these references. Yet surely Loisy was right in implying that there is no overwhelming certainty about Mary of the historic kind in respect to her birth, which can be found in considerable measure in the Gospels of Matthew, Mark and Luke. Of course even that reporting about Jesus comes to us in a way that makes ascription of precise historical accuracy dubious. It is all based upon oral traditions, handed on from place to place and community to community, perhaps even from person to person, until finally it reached redactors or editorial hands – whether or not before their efforts there was *some* writing which provided written material that they could use and arrange – which collected and transcribed what they had available and so produced the three books which in the New Testament are called by the names of 'the evangelists', Matthew, Mark and Luke.

I have excluded John's Gospel at this point because biblical scholars agree that it belongs in a somewhat different category from the other three Gospels, although it too is made up of bits of material which have been arranged according to an easily discernible pattern and which (as is increasingly recognized by scholars) doubtless rests back upon some series of oral traditions presumably known independently of those behind the first three (or synoptic) Gospels. None the less, when we come to consider what in fact is to be found in the New Testament about St Mary, it will of course be necessary for us to include the material from the fourth Gospel.

But before we proceed further it is important to understand how we can best approach the Gospel stories. We must reiterate that today we can no longer regard them as if they were straight historical reporting. To see why, we do not need to sketch the development of New Testament studies during the past century and particularly within the past half-century. The reader will find an account in the many books which offer 'introductions' to biblical study, perhaps most widely available in such volumes as the *Interpreter's Bible* (Abingdon Press, Nashville, USA) or in the many popular biblical studies which have appeared recently from the Oxford and Cambridge University presses in England, and from other publishers. It will suffice to state quite simply that thanks to historical criticism, synoptic and literary criticism, more recent 'form-criticism' and 'redaction criticism', in all their variety, there is today a general scholarly agreement about the nature of the Gospels and about how best they may be read and studied.

Briefly then, the Gospels are 'witnesses' to the apostolic faith, written – like the earlier material upon which they were based and which they communicated – to awaken or deepen the conviction of the earliest Christian believers that in the event we indicate when we say 'Jesus Christ' there was a signal 'act of God' taking place in a human activity, an act such that the divine reality was there both disclosed, revealed and released as divine energy for humankind. The stories found in the Gospels are told 'from faith to faith', as St Paul put it in a different connection. They are *from* those who already were convinced believers and members of the earliest Christian fellowship and they are *to* those who were either beginners in the faith or who wished for some reason to be informed more fully about what had taken place to establish this proclamation as historically grounded and not simply a product of human imagination or speculation. What is told about the mother of Jesus is in the same case as the other Gospel narratives. It is part of the total witness although of course it plays nothing like so significant a role in the whole complex as does that which is said about Jesus himself.

But this approach to the Gospels does not make what is said unimportant or misleading. Essentially what it requires from us is a shift of stance, *from* one that could and did assume possession of strictly factual data *to* one in which whatever data we possess are mediated to us through (and in terms of) the apostolic faith. Behind this we cannot go with any certainty, even if some scholars (like the German Willi Marxsen) are prepared to seek for and (in their opinion) to find clear traces of even more primitive material. If that is indeed the case, even then the material used must first have been oral rather than anything resembling the kind of written historical reportage which in our own day, and even in an earlier age when 'accurate history' first began to be valued, might be expected. Much the same is true, of course, for the Old Testament. Indeed it was the scholarly study of that part of the Bible which inaugurated the newer way of looking at the New Testament narratives, of interpreting their significance, and understanding whatever historical validity was to be found in them.

Unquestionably, conservatively-minded Christians, above

3

all those who insist on the 'inerrancy of scripture' even if they are not 'literalistic' in their understanding of it, will regard what has just been said as destructive of faith. They will denounce the whole enterprise as 'radical' in a pejorative sense of that word. To them it will be the work of sceptics and unbelievers and will amount to nothing less than denial of what for centuries has been taken as authentic Christian faith. I shall not endeavour here to respond to those who take this view; I need only refer the reader to fairly recent books like *Fundamentalism* by James Barr (SCM Press, second edition 1981) which deal with the subject and which show, convincingly to my mind, that the approach to the scriptures roughly outlined above is very far from being entirely negative and destructive. Rather, in my view (as in that of others who are not in the biblicist-literalist groups) it opens up a new but also a valid way of reading those scriptures. That way has the great virtue of applying the method suggested in a famous saying of Benjamin Jowett, that 'we are to read the Bible as we would any other book' with the end-result that we shall come to see that what the Bible has to tell us is *not* what we find in 'any other book' but yet is of enormous significance; and that it can make an equally enormous difference in how we look at God, the world, and our human existence. What is more, it can do this in a fashion which is not a denial or contradiction of the rest of our human knowledge about the world and ourselves – and through that give us some knowledge about God too.

The way, then, in which we can properly study the material in the Gospels (and, to take another instance, in the Acts of the Apostles) is not the way in which we might read a typical piece of precise historical narrative. What we must do is first to consider why this or that particular piece of oral tradition was valued and why later it was set down in writing, and what was its part and place in the early communication of faith in the central figure Jesus, about whom this tradition was concerned and towards awakening a responding faith in whom this tradition had its central place.

With all this in mind, we may now turn to the places in the Gospels where Mary is mentioned. Certainly there *are* not many of them; but equally certainly they are present in the Gospels and they should be studied with care.

The first two chapters of both Matthew and Luke are often called 'the nativity stories'. They are found in Matt. 1.18-2.23 and Luke 1.26-2.52. There is no need to repeat here what they say; the reader can turn to them in his or her New Testament. In the Lukan material, the particular point of interest for us is the account of the so-called Annunciation, which we shall consider in the next chapter, with its centring of attention on the way in which the future mother of Jesus is 'told of her destiny by an angel' and in which she is represented as accepting that destiny with humility and obedience. Elsewhere in the Lukan narratives there is the statement that while she was 'espoused' (we should say 'engaged') to marry a man called Joseph, she and he had not yet 'come together' – that is, engaged in sexual relations. The rest of the nativity chapters in Luke are filled with details obviously legendary, such as the coming of the shepherds to see the new-born babe 'lying in a manger' or stable-stall, because his family, who we are told had come to Bethlehem for the purpose of a government census, could find no 'room in the inn'. Mary, 'great with child', was therefore obliged to give birth in very humble surroundings. The *implication* of the material in these Lukan narratives is that her child was miraculously conceived, although only two verses in Luke appear to require such an interpretation (1.34-35) and some scholars have regarded them as later interpolations.

In Matt. 1.18-21 a similar emphasis is found. Joseph learns 'in a dream' that his future wife is to bear a son 'conceived in her by the Holy Spirit'; while the material also suggests that Joseph did not yet 'know her' (have sexual relations with her) and presumably waited for this until she had brought forth this 'first-born son'. A prophecy from Isaiah is quoted; it is the passage in which the prophet speaks about 'a virgin' who is to bring forth a son as a sign of the divine favour for God's people. As it happens, the text in Isaiah does *not* in fact speak of a 'virgin' but rather of a 'young woman'. All Old Testament scholars agree here that the Greek word *parthenos* or 'virgin' is an inaccurate translation of the original Hebrew in the prophet's oracle, where the inference is only that a young woman will soon have a child as a sign of God's goodwill to his 'chosen people'.

What are we to make of this material, taken along with the other bits found in the first two chapters of Matthew and Luke? I believe that we can best understand it as essentially having to do, not with a biological miracle (although this idea may very well have been in the minds of those who set it down), but with the conviction that in the coming of Jesus into the world there was a prevenience of God and an 'over-ruling' of events by divine providence. Thus the One in whom the primitive Christian fellowship centred its faith was not the accidental appearance of another man in the world, but was to be seen as part of (and indeed integral to) God's loving purpose for humankind. In other words, the narratives are concerned to affirm Jesus as genuinely 'from God' rather than to assert the supposed virginity of his mother.

The other references in these four chapters from Matthew and Luke have to do with a trip which the 'holy family' is said to have made into Egypt to escape from King Herod's attempt at assassination; the visit of the family to Jerusalem where Jesus encountered Jewish elders in the Temple and both 'heard them and asked them questions': the return of the family to Nazareth; and with the way in which Jesus was 'subject' to Joseph and Mary. We are told that as Mary thought about what had happened 'she kept all these sayings in her heart' while Jesus himself 'increased in wisdom and stature, and in favour with God and man'. The main interest is in Jesus and what happened to him as well as in what he himself did. Yet Mary plays her part as a loving and devoted mother to her son. She is in the picture; yet her role in it is not the main interest.

Elsewhere in the first three Gospels there are other and occasional references to Mary. An example is when she and other members of the family sought Jesus to urge him to give up the ministry which he had undertaken. They thought, we are told, that he was 'beside himself' – not quite in his right mind, as we might put it – because the way in which he taught and acted created something of a sensation and aroused sufficient antipathy from Jewish leadership to put his life in peril. Interestingly enough, Jesus' response here is to include within his family *all* those who listen to him – '*these* are my mother and my brethren, who hear the word of God and do it' (Luke 8.19-21, with its parallel in Matt. 12.47-50). It would seem quite likely that this particular reference has some foundation in genuine historical recollection, although the use made of it indicates that for the two evangelists its intention is probably to claim for Jesus' followers – both initially and in later years – a real place in that 'extended family'.

Before we go on to speak of the Johannine references to Mary, it will be useful to remark that doubtless most if not all of the material so far considered, and certainly the material found in the two opening chapters of Matthew and Luke, belongs to the genre which in traditional Hebrew thinking and speaking was known as *haggadah*. This latter is to be distinguished from *halakah*, which is straightforward moral teaching. Essentially *haggadah* is the use of a significant story of the sort that Italians indicate when they say of a report that it is *ben trovato*. It is both apt and appropriate to communicate a profound and important truth about God and God's way with men and women. In Jewish writing generally, as also in the oral communication which often may have preceded it, the specific historicity of the story is not the big matter. The main interest is in the truth that is being communicated, the message being proclaimed, and the response that is to be expected to the message. We have already seen something of this sort in our discussion of the nativity stories. It may be true also of the kind of incidents to which we have just made reference, although there is no reason to doubt that some factual happening probably lies behind that material. In any event my earlier comment still holds: the reason for the presence of such narratives or incidents is not what we today would call straightforward historical concern but rather to express a faith, which will in turn evoke a faith, in the One who is at the centre of the story.

In the Fourth Gospel, the principal places where Mary makes her appearance are at the wedding-feast at Cana of Galilee (John 2.1-12) and at the cross on Calvary (John 19.25-27). In respect of the former, it is important for us to notice that this is one of the 'signs' (*semeia* in the Greek, incorrectly translated in older English versions of the Bible as 'miracle') which Jesus is believed to have performed as 'enacted expressions of truth' about God and humankind.

In the Cana story, where Jesus turns water into wine, the purpose seems clearly to communicate the profound reality of Christian life in grace made possible through the Lord himself, so that the 'water' of ordinary Jewish existence as God's 'chosen people' becomes the 'wine' of new life in God made available through the event of Jesus Christ. Mary's part in the story is simply her presence at the wedding-feast and her informing Jesus that 'they have no wine' with Jesus'

8

response that this is not her business ('Woman, what have I to do with you? Mine hour is not yet come' – the use of 'woman' here is not originally pejorative, as it seems in English), followed by Mary's telling the servants at the feast that they are to 'do whatsoever he (Jesus) says to them'.

In the part of the Fourth Gospel which places Mary at the scene of the crucifixion, we have the little incident in which as she 'stood by the cross of Jesus', her son 'saw his mother with the disciple whom he loved (presumably John) standing by'. He said to her, 'Woman, behold your son' and to the disciple 'Behold your mother'. 'And from that hour,' the story concludes, 'that disciple took her into his own home.' If the view of a number of contemporary scholars is accepted – and there seems every reason to accept it – that the Fourth Gospel includes some traditional historical material not present in the first three Gospels, we may well believe that there is here a genuine recollection which was first repeated orally and eventually found its way into the compilation of that Gospel.

The last biblical reference to Mary to which we may now attend is not in the Gospels but in the Acts of the Apostles (1.14), where we are told that the first group of Christian believers, after the resurrection of Jesus and his being 'received in a cloud out of (their) sight', included among them 'Mary the mother of Jesus' along with 'his brethren' and with 'the women' who had become part of the company of believers in the risen and ascended Lord. Acts is generally regarded by scholars as 'the second volume' of a book of 'memoirs' and hence the story of the primitive Christian fellowship, written by 'Luke' (the first volume of which is his Gospel). There seems no reason why that writer did not have available to him information about the first days of the Christian church and we may very well conclude that here too we have a bit of historical recollection. Otherwise it would be hard to see the point of the reference. No obvious affirmation of faith is present beyond the insistence that the very earliest post-resurrection fellowship 'continued with one accord in prayer and supplication', as the verse immediately before the one cited states.

This is practically all that we can say about the 'historical' data – and I have put the adjective in inverted commas because I wish to indicate once again the way in which such data must be understood in the light of informed New Testament study. We now turn to material about Mary which may be called 'myth'; and we are at once confronted by a considerable mass of references which belong in the category of apocryphal or pseudepigraphical literature. I shall not discuss this non-biblical material at any length. It is to be found collected in such books as have been translated in M. R. James' *The Apocryphal New Testament*, first published in 1924 and reprinted many times. Here we have the *Infancy Gospel of Thomas*, the Arabic *Gospel of the Childhood*, the *History of Joseph the Carpenter*, and the *Protoevangelium of James*. What is present in all these documents is indeed 'apocryphal' in that it is obviously not based upon reliable or even probable historical data. It is the production of a devout but highly fanciful imagination, whose details are of no significance for Christian faith but which are rather an embroidering of that faith, often with outlandish improbabilities – as, for example, the account of the midwife's presence at Jesus' birth, not to speak of the story that the young Jesus turned clay-pigeons into birds or that as a child he rounded with destructive effect upon some of his playmates when they had displeased him.

Such stories are hardly to be classified as proper mythological literature. Rather, they belong to sheer legend of a sort that has nothing to commend it; and we may disregard them in a serious attempt to look at the development of *genuine* myth about the mother of Jesus.

To the latter category belongs such material as the

10

interpretation of Mary as 'the second Eve'. This notion is found as early as Justin Martyr in the second century and in St Irenaeus and Tertullian soon afterwards. Here her obedience is said to reverse the disobedience of the original Eve, by whose choice humankind 'fell' from pristine righteousness. Again, we have Mary's 'perpetual virginity' which was first enunciated in the apocryphal *Protoevangelium* (mentioned above) but *possibly* taught also by Irenaeus and Clement of Alexandria and later plainly asserted by Athanasius, who indeed used the exact Greek word *aeiparthenos*. Again, 'the bodily assumption' of Mary into heaven was taught plainly by Gregory of Tours in the late sixth century, although intimations of it are present earlier in the apocryphal material. Of course it was only as late as 1950 that Pope Pius XII made this belief in a 'bodily assumption' an article of faith for the Roman Catholic Church, even if the 'Dormition' or 'Falling Asleep' of St Mary had for centuries been taught in the Eastern Orthodox churches.

On the other hand, Mary was for centuries said by some theologians to be 'immaculately conceived' – that is, without her sharing in original sin. This latter remained a subject much disputed within the Western church and it was not until 1854 that it received for Roman Catholics the status of a defined and imposed dogma under Pope Pius IX. – His bull *Ineffabilis deus* says that 'the Blessed Virgin Mary, in the first moment of her conception, by a singular grace and privilege of Almighty God, in virtue of the merits of Jesus Christ the Saviour of mankind, was preserved immune from every stain of original sin'. Eastern Orthodox Christians have not accepted this doctrine as it stands, although they *have* been prepared to speak of Mary as 'immaculate', which for them presumably means that in her own decisions and actions she was in fact 'sinless'.

Mariological mythology has also included other

11

developments, such as the fairly recent Roman Catholic argument for her role as a co-operant agent in human redemption along with her son. In such circles there is talk about her being 'co-redemptrix', although Vatican II was more temperate in these respects. In that council's *Dogmatic Constitution on the Church* there is a chapter which places Mary *within* the church, seeing her as one who is redeemed and a member of the mystical body of Christ. At the same time, she is styled 'the Mother' of Christians; and when Pope Paul VI promulgated that Constitution he explicitly spoke of her as 'the Mother of the Church'.

In Protestant circles, of course, mariological doctrines have been denied or much reduced, although the reformer John Calvin could speak of her in the highest terms. Anglicans generally have been reserved but not so negative. Indeed the Caroline divines of the seventeenth century spoke of Mary's holiness, and one of Bishop Ken's hymns calls her 'the temple' which God built for the express purpose of sending the Son into the world. In the Tractarian Movement's successor, Anglo-Catholicism, the devout theologian Charles Gore once said that we are to pay to Mary 'all veneration short of worship'. Interestingly enough, it might also be observed that today in some Reformed Church circles there is a new openness to mariological thought. Max Thurian of Taizè in a recent book on *The Virgin Mary* commended a 'chastened' devotion to her, speaking as he did from within the Taizè community with its enormous respect for the Catholic tradition.

During the long period of christological controversy in the early church the term *theotokos* ('bearer of God', often and not accurately translated as 'Mother of God') came to be used of Mary. The Antiochene theologians generally rejected this term, which had been in common use in many parts of the Christian world before the Council of Chalcedon in AD 451. The Antiochenes preferred to speak of Mary as *christotokos*, 'the bearer of Christ', since to them the other term suggested absurdly and blasphemously that *God* had 'a mother' – although of course they were quite ready to affirm that the manhood of Jesus which God the Word had 'assumed' by incarnation was born of Mary. At this point an important christological issue is raised; we shall speak about it in a succeeding chapter.

The present chapter has attempted to indicate what historical data we possess and how that data may best be understood. It has also given a very brief mention of the development of mariological mythology. With the material discussed here constantly in mind, what can we say as contemporary Christians about the place of Mary in the continuing faith, worship and life of Christian people? In the next chapters we shall begin our discussion of a possible answer to this question.

2

'Be it Unto Me' – the Consent of Mary

We have seen that a large amount of non-historical material has been added to the little we can know with historic certainty about the mother of Jesus. That she *was* his mother is clear enough, that she must have cared for him as an infant and as a child is obvious. It may even be true that she was with him on a number of later occasions and that she was among those who were at Calvary when he was crucified. But beyond that, we have to recognize that much of the material about Mary in the Gospels – and certainly in the story of the marriage feast at Cana – is not historically secure, although of course some of the references which we have mentioned may have had an historical basis.

When we come to what I have suggested might be called 'the myth' in which Mary plays a significant role, we are in a different realm. Here pious imagination seems on occasion to have run riot and become what may be called 'legend'. There is little if any likelihood that what is told in the apocryphal gospels belongs to any type of narrative save that of sheer legend. As the stories pile up we see emerging a highly fanciful conception of Mary and of her relationship with her son, giving her an important part in the post-resurrection Christian community; and of course most of all, in the relatively late 'account' of her death and heavenly 'assumption'.

Yet we must also remember that myth need not necessarily

be only a fanciful creation which bears no relationship whatever to genuine religious faith. Sheer uncontrolled imagination can get to work here, to be sure. But as G.B. Shaw has Joan of Arc say on one occasion in his play about her, maybe imagination is 'the way', or a way, in which God speaks to men and women. Or to put it in another fashion, imagination may have the capacity to open up realms of human possibility, suggest important aspects of religious truth and disclose something enduringly valid about God and God's relationship with humankind.

What follows in this chapter will single out one point which has profound theological importance and is relevant to any devout response to what Christians believe God did in the event of Jesus Christ. In succeeding chapters other significant points will be discussed.

In classical Catholic theology the mother of Jesus has been called 'the consenting cause of the Incarnation'. St Thomas Aquinas, the supreme exponent of such classical theology, dwells on this topic, making the conception and birth of Jesus not only the act of God but also including the act of a human being. His insistence is that for God to have become 'incarnate', to be 'made flesh' in a truly human life, it was essential that from the human side there should be a genuine positive response to the divine initiative. In classical terms that initiative was 'prevenient' or prior to the response; but *both* initiative and response were necessarily involved. The Gospel narrative which makes this clear to St Thomas and other Catholic theologians is the story of the annunciation in Luke's Gospel, in which we are told both of the appearance to St Mary of an angel who informed her that in God's purpose she was intended to be the mother of the promised One, and also the reply to that announcement made by St Mary: 'Be it unto me according to thy word.'

The account of the incident is found as I have said in Luke's Gospel, 1.26 and following. In the Revised Standard

Version of the Bible we read that Mary is told, 'You have found favour with God. And behold, you will conceive in your womb, and bear a son, and you shall call his name Jesus. He will be great, and will be called the Son of the Most High: and the Lord God will give him the throne of his father David, and he will reign over the house of Jacob for ever; and of his kingdom there shall be no end.' When Mary hears this announcement she asks, 'How can this be, since I have no husband?' And the angel answers her by saying that the Holy Spirit will come upon [her] and the power of the Most High will overshadow [her]; therefore the child to be born [of her] will be called holy, the Son of God. Then comes Mary's response, 'Behold I am the handmaid of the Lord; let it be to me according to your word.'

In the lections appointed for the Feast of the Annunciation (25 March) in the Alternative Service Book of the Church of England, this 'gospel for the day' is accompanied by a reading from the Old Testament, Isaiah 52.7-10, and an 'epistle for the day' from the New Testament, Galatians 4.1-5. The former of course is Isaiah's prophecy of the care which will be shown by God to 'his people', in that 'the Lord has bared his holy arm in the sight of all nations, and the whole world from end to end shall see the deliverance of our God' (New English Bible text). The appointed 'epistle' is St Paul's declaration that this prophecy has now been fulfilled, since 'when the time had fully come, God sent forth his Son, born of woman, born under the Law, to redeem those who were under the Law, so that we might receive adoption as sons' (Revised Standard Version text). The 'introductory sentence' provided in that Prayer Book for the Feast is this: 'A virgin shall conceive and bear a son, and his name shall be called Emmanuel, God-with-us' (Matt. 1.23, repeating the words as given in Isa. 7.14). The 'post-communion sentence' for the eucharist on that day is John's text, 'The Word was made flesh, and lived among us' (John 1.14).

16

Thus in the readings and the other material appointed for that traditional feast, as well as in the familiar collect which speaks of our knowing 'the incarnation of [God's] Son Jesus Christ by the message of an angel', there is an explicit connection established between the annunciation story and the coming of Jesus as the 'incarnate Son of God'. Although this is not said in so many words, the implication is precisely that which, as I have noted above, has been present in classical Catholic theology: that Mary was the human agent whose response in faith and whose obedience to the message of the angel were essential if God was to do what in Christian faith God is believed to have done.

In considering this affirmation we need to attend to several relevant matters. One is the significance of 'incarnation'. Certainly that is the traditional word to describe what the Christian church affirms about Jesus Christ. The word has been hallowed by long usage and is assumed by many (although of course not by all) Christian thinkers to be the only way in which to speak properly when we are talking about Jesus Christ. He is 'the incarnate God'; in him there is the 'making flesh' [or human] of the Word or *Logos* of God, so that here 'God's presence and his very self' – as Cardinal Newman's hymn phrases it – are with us in human terms. Yet it may very well be the case that this 'incarnation' idiom is associated with patterns of thought which are by no means absolute. It may be the case that another way of affirming the importance and significance of Jesus could be found which would neither deny nor reduce the point of the ancient formula but would express in more contemporary idiom what that formula was attempting to assert. This is not the place to develop an alternative idiom. Suffice it to say that a good deal of present-day theology has been concerned to work out precisely such a possible contemporary expression of the importance and significance of Jesus. An effort is made in such theology to show how we may better understand, and convey in a different idiom, the Christian conviction that somehow in the event we indicate when we say 'Jesus Christ' there has been a focal and decisive activity of God which we Christians have been brought to see and believe, and which makes a profound difference in the affairs of humankind and which is an action of God and in a fully human existence with all that existence's limitations and conditions.

A second point to be considered here is the set of ideas behind mediaeval talk about 'consenting cause'. Here we have to do with the belief that the ultimate causative principle or agency in the creation is indeed God, but that in human affairs God works in and through genuine human causation. Thus God respects and values human dignity and responsibility and does not smash through or disregard them in divine activity in the world.

For St Thomas, this rested back upon his acceptance of the Aristotelian view that there are four kinds of cause: material, instrumental or efficient, formal and final. A simple illustration makes this clear. A house is being built. Its *material* cause is the stone or timber which is used; its *instrumental or efficient* cause is the labour which is involved in doing the building; its *formal* cause is the plan or design which an architect has made and a builder is to follow; and its *final* cause is the purpose or intention of the job, which is of course to build a dwelling in which humans may have their abode. In respect to the divine activity in the world, the final cause is God's intention or purpose; the material cause is the creaturely stuff which God uses; the efficient cause is the natural or human agency which is required for the task: and the formal cause is the basic understanding of exactly what this or that particular entity in the creation is in itself, and what makes it precisely that entity.

The relevant point here is simply to ask to what extent and

in what manner 'consent' may be given by the creature to the prevenient and initiating activity of God. Obviously St Thomas, along with all who have spoken for classical theology during the centuries before the emergence of biblical critical study, assumed that the material we read in the annunciation narrative was reliably historical in nature. Furthermore, he naturally assumed that St Mary, in making her reported response to the angel's message, was well aware of what she was saying – she accepted that she was to conceive and bear a child who would indeed be 'the Son of the Most High', as the fulfilment of prophetic utterance, and the One of whose 'kingdom there would be no end'.

In the light of New Testament study over the past century, however, we can no longer think that the annunciation story represents this kind of straightforward historical reporting. In one way or another most scholars interpret the story as more in the realm of imaginative discourse than as explicit factual material. Furthermore, it is difficult for us to see how St Mary, even if the story should be historical, even if it does not belong in the realm of imaginative literature, could have had any conscious awareness of the ultimate significance of what was told her. Whence her response could not have been a plain and simple 'Yes' to an equally plain statement of divine purpose as spoken by the angel.

Does this mean, then, that we are dealing here with material that is merely fanciful? Or is it possible to interpret it in such a fashion that it represents, in its own particular way, a profound and inescapable Christian truth? Here we come to see the importance of what was said in the opening chapter about the value, indeed the validity, of much that is certainly mythical in nature. The annunciation story may be dubiously historical both in detail and in background. Yet perhaps it is telling us something that within the Christian tradition of faith, worship and life is of quite enormous significance. It is vividly presenting in story form (like older

19

Jewish *haggadah*) a truth which Christian people must regard as integral to their very existence as humans living in a created order, but who also believe that in and behind that created order there is a supreme, dependable, worshipful and unsurpassable reality from whom all things come and who in a real sense is the 'sovereign ruler' or governor of the world. I believe this is the case. I shall now attempt to explain the sense in which it is the case, with its relevance for Christians today, just as it also had its significance in past ages of the tradition of which we are part and in which we live.

In my view the best conceptuality for use in discussing such questions is the one known as 'Process Thought'. My reason for saying this will be apparent in the sequel. But first it is necessary to give a very brief (and therefore inadequate) summary of the main emphases in that conceptuality. For more detailed exposition I refer the reader to my *The Lure of Divine Love*, in which there is a fairly complete presentation; or to my book *Picturing God*, in which there are several chapters which are relevant to the present discussion.

The Process conceptuality may be summed up under six headings to which I now turn. First, our world is in process or change; it is not a static or fixed creation. Things are on the move – not necessarily for the better, yet none the less they do not 'continue in one stay', for ours is an evolutionary world. Second, the constituents of such a world are not 'things' or entities of a fixed sort; they are events or happenings, with an objective reality but also with an internal or subjective experiential quality. This does not mean that all such events are conscious in our human sense, but rather that each of them has a subjectivity integral to it, quite as much as its objective *thereness*. Third, everything in the world is in relationship with everything else, so that what happens *here* has its influence or effect on what happens *there*. Reality is societal or (to use Whitehead's word) 'organismic'. Hence the created world is more like what we know in our human body than like what we know of machines or organizational groups. Fourth, in that world there is a certain freedom of decision, varying in intensity at different levels, with consequences that follow from decisions which have been taken by the constituent entities. Thanks to that factor, novelties emerge as an event or occasion decides for new possibilities presented to it and 'prehended' or grasped by it. At the same time there is an over-all continuity so that we cannot speak meaningfully of intrusions into the creation as it were 'from outside'. There is genuine newness, to be sure; but this does not imply external intervention from a supposed non-worldly outside being. Fifth, in the long run persuasive rather than coercive exercise of creative power is more effectual and enduring – the really strong exercise of power is not the coercion which so often we think to be the case (and which indeed often seems in fact to be the case) but it is rather the slower, more intimate and alluring quality that solicits and may receive a response which produces significant results. Sixth, whatever we may wish to say about deity – the supreme, worshipful, dependable and unsurpassable reality in and behind and through all things (unsurpassable, that is, by anything not itself, yet open to the possibility of 'excelling itself' in succeeding stages of process) – cannot be conceived as the sheer contradiction of the preceding five principles but rather is to be taken in Whitehead's phrase as their 'chief exemplification'. This does not imply that deity is only creation writ large; rather it is an affirmation that deity is not the total denial of such explanatory principles as have been found necessary to interpret experience both human and natural. Obviously God cannot be spoken of as if deity were identical with the non-divine; and the ordering of the necessary principles may be different in God than in creaturely occasions. Nevertheless what is to be said about God is not a 'sheer anomaly' but will be congruous with natural or human events. As classical theology would put it, there are *vestigia dei* ('traces of God') in the creation, although in the process perspective it might better be stated in a reverse fashion – that in and with deity there are parallels or similarities with what we ourselves know, feel and experience.

I apologize for the above long paragraph of explanation. It will soon be seen how important what has just been said is for our main topic in this chapter, providing as it does a context which helps to make good sense of talk about 'consenting cause' in respect to divine activity in the world.

That point can be put in a single sentence which must then be developed more fully. The sentence is this: '*All* divine activity in the created order is effected through agencies that are creaturely and that at the human level are humanly undertaken.' In conventional Christian idiom, then, this is to be seen as an 'incarnational' or 'sacramental' world, in which one reality (God) operates through and by means of another reality (the natural or human). Only in that fashion do we 'know' God. Only in that way are we brought into contact with the divine activity.

It is like our human awareness of beauty, which we can grasp only in and by seeing beautiful persons, things, portraiture and the like. So also we know goodness only in and by seeing good deeds or good persons or enriching kinds of experience. We can grasp the meaning of justice only through awareness of just or righteous actions and concerns. Like all these, deity is made available to us humans in and by that which takes place on our own level of experience. This is the given and necessary condition and means through which, and through which alone, creatures like us men and women can grasp and be grasped by that which is non-human and transcendent of ordinary created 'things' – the truly supreme, adorable, worshipful and entirely dependable reality of God. To put it almost too bluntly, God *cannot* act towards and in the world save in this fashion; this is the condition with which and to which deity must inevitably accommodate itself.

I quite realize that to some persons such a statement will seem seriously wrong so far as Christian faith is concerned. It will be said that it amounts to a flat denial of genuine theism. To this my response is that it is indeed a denial of the residual *deism* which persists in so many minds, as if God were a remote creator who once started things on their course but now is active in the creation only by intrusive or interventionary acts. It is indeed a denial of such deism; but it is also a rejection of the supposed alternative of pantheism, in which God is simply identified with creation – Spinoza's *deus sive natura*. In truth it is a pan*en*theistic view (I italize the '*en*' to make the point), in which all created occasions are 'in' God and God is 'in' them, so that through them and by them we come to respond to an omnipresent divine operation, with its several differing intensities and with its varying modes of expression. Ours is not a uniformitarian creation; it has its ups and downs, its more or less. And the central Christian affirmation, as I understand it, is simply that in a world like that, the event known as Jesus Christ is the place where we have been given a peculiarly vivid and decisive revelation of deity, accompanied by a peculiarly intensive release of divine energy. Here there is a disclosure of God as 'pure unbounded Love' with a release into the creation of the divine power of that love; and this is 'for us and for our salvation', as the Nicene Creed asserts.

What the story of the annunciation tells us can be understood in precisely this context. Since all divine activity in the creation is dependent upon the presence of creaturely responsivity to divine invitation or solicitation or lure (call it what you will), this focal instance of that activity could not have occurred if there had not been a readiness, on the part of a human agent, to say 'Yes'. Most often in human experience such a response is not vivid and highly conscious. When I respond to the lure of beauty as I meet its various manifestations, or to goodness when I see it in this or that instance, or to justice when it is brought to my attention by specific righteous persons or deeds, I may not be in the position to affirm that I have a deep awareness of what is going on. None the less, this is the way in which I make the beauty or goodness or justice my own: I have answered affirmatively to what is disclosed in such moments. Nor need I always be able to say, what as a genuine theist I must eventually say, that here God is supremely at work towards men and women in the world. God is often known through what Baron von Hügel years ago taught us to call 'secular incognitos' or what Whitehead spoke about as 'the secular functioning' of deity.

Yet there *can* be moments or occasions when there is a more vivid and more conscious awareness. Whatever is the sense in which this can be said about the response of Mary to whatever may have elicited in her human experience a readiness to 'consent' to the divine initiative, or even whether there was indeed any such vivid conscious response in her 'consent', this does not reduce nor deny the reality in question. Thus the story of the Annunciation can well serve us as the scriptural witness to a response made to the divine invitation, however that may be interpreted. The insight of classical theology at this point was correct. Furthermore, I suggest that it entails for the rest of us a similar readiness to say our 'yes' to whatever of God has been intimated in our experience. If Mary's 'Be it unto me according to your word' represents a signal expression of 'consent', our own response to God is also to be an expression of that same kind of human experience.

We may not find it helpful to use the Thomist phrase

24

about 'consenting cause of the Incarnation'. Perhaps we can find, or try to find, some other way of putting it into words. Yet what is here being declared seems to be an essential truth. God waits upon human – or in other levels of creation, upon some natural – willingness to co-operate with the divine purpose in the world. God does not force upon us, through a coercive act, what gives life significance, value and meaning. God's power is the power of persuasive love, offering a lure which can entice us and then bring about our enrichment and empowerment. For unlike our all-too-human tendency to drive or compel, which in the long run often accomplishes the exact opposite of what we wish or intend, God moves more tenderly and gently and in the long run much more 'compellingly'. The divine 'compulsion' is not that of force as a power over-riding creaturely freedom and responsibility. Rather, it is the 'compulsion' of love-in-act. Elsewhere I have quoted a splendid sentence from the Greek tragedian Sophocles, that in human affairs 'the final word is love'; and I end this chapter by saying that if a Greek dramatist could make such a statement, a Christian believer not only can but must make it with even deeper conviction.

Love: that is what God is, that is what God does, that is how God deals with us. Even the divine judgment or appraisal is in such terms – as St John of the Cross said, 'At the evening of our day we shall be judged by love.' Love never coerces. Love always asks a response. Love always waits upon consent. So it is that we can find great meaning in the central point of the annunciation story. So it is that I, for one, can see in the mother of Jesus, about whom we know so little in terms of strict history, precisely a supreme symbolic instance of consent to the divine will. So it is that I, for one, can honour the mother of the Lord as she has been portrayed for us in tales that may indeed lack strict historical accuracy but that yet convey a profound and, for a Christian, an inescapable truth.

that part of his kenosis that requires
our 'Yes' to him.

'And Mary said, "Be it unto me according to your word."' As we shall see in the next chapter, this makes her a model for all genuine Christian discipleship. In that sense, granted the slight historical material and the large amount of myth, she may still properly be styled 'the mother of us all' – that is of all who are members of the living community of Christian faith and worship and life.

3

Model for Christian Discipleship

I have said that we have very slight or 'primitive' historical data about the life of Mary. Yet what we *do* have tells us that in the earliest Christian tradition she was always portrayed as faithful, hopeful and loving. I urge that we should take seriously both this historical material and the myth which in the ongoing tradition has grown up about Mary. We cannot dismiss all this as just so much fantasy. *Something* is being said here: and that something has its importance in our total understanding of the role which the mother of Jesus has been seen to occupy. Granted that this can only be grasped with the use of the sanctified imagination; yet to say that this is the case does not reduce everything said about her to the realm of the fairy-tale whose only value would be that it tells an agreeable story, or amuses, or just possibly may edify. I suggest that we cannot disregard in a cavalier fashion how the living Christian tradition has found itself led to speak of Mary.

So we must consider Mary's role in that tradition. I do not for a moment claim that this role of Mary, such as I am defending, can be demonstrated by the evidence, historical or in terms of mythical discourse, which is available for us. I am only stating that this role is congruous with the material. There is no need to reject out of hand what the living tradition has consistently asserted for many centuries.

One part of Mary's faith, or better her faithfulness, is reflected in the story told in Luke's Gospel about her response to the message of the angel. We do not need to accept that story historically at its face value. Indeed, in view of what we know about those first two chapters in Luke as early Christian *haggadah*, such acceptance is impossible. On the other hand, there is no reason to doubt that from the time of her conception of Jesus Mary was a person of faith. She did not know what her son was later to be taken by Christians to be; neither did she know what was his particular vocation in the divine-human economy. Yet as a mother whose son himself was a man of faith, we can see that her attitude and her way of behaving was of the sort which follows when we recognize that a son is influenced and affected by his parents and above all by his mother.

Incidentally, something also needs to be said here about the part which Joseph, Mary's husband, must have played in the upbringing of Jesus. Someone has remarked that Joseph is the 'forgotten man' in the story; but he is portrayed as trusting in God and as prepared to accept what he believed to be God's will. If Joseph was Jesus' human father – and there is no reason, theologically or otherwise, to question this – then his paternal care must have been notable, even if lacking the intensity which is more often found in the feminine parent. Indeed if he were only 'foster-father', as conventional orthodoxy readily grants, his influence must have been significant. The story of Jesus' 'miraculous conception' as found in the Gospel tales in Matthew and Luke is not an historical or biological matter, but has a theological point: Jesus is from God as well as from humankind. And the human side included the part played by Joseph as well as that of Mary.

If Mary was faithful in her care for her son, so also she is said to have lived in hopefulness. As a devout Jewish maiden she shared naturally and inevitably in the Jewish expectation that God would so act in the realm of human affairs that right human existence might be made possible. The hope was expressed in all Jewish religious belief and practice. Since Mary belonged to what were known as 'the people of the land' she would have been loyal to what the Jewish tradition taught about God. Doubtless she would have engaged in the regular worship at the synagogue in Nazareth and with her husband would have brought her son to share in that worship. Joseph himself was a *tekton* (which means *not* 'carpenter' [as our translations give it] but a village artisan). Doubtless Jesus was under Joseph's guidance and grew up to work in that kind of job for many years until he experienced the vivid sense of a calling to 'proclaim the kingdom of God' and to preach the necessity of repentance before that kingdom's coming. The deep hope or expectation in which a Jewish boy was brought up would play its part in all this; and we may suppose that Mary helped in this development, even if she and others in Jesus' family seem not to have understood in any deep sense her son's vocation.

Yet if she did not understand she did love her son as a faithful Jewish mother – and presumably that loving was also part of her continuing relationship with Jesus as he grew from infancy through adolescence to maturity. The portrayal of this relationship of love in great art and poetry is very moving; artists seem to have felt deeply about it, particularly in their portrayal of mother and child. They catch the spirit of concern and guardianship with remarkable felicity and they enable us to respond deeply to this aspect of her attitude and action.

Here also we may remember the way in which the insight of present-day experts in child nurture has enabled us to see more clearly how faith, hope and love would have been nurtured in Jesus himself. Humanly speaking he owed almost everything initially to his parental associations; and his deepening of what he had learned would be a natural process towards the fulfilling of his vocation once he had come to understand what that meant and what it involved. For we should remember that so far as our evidence goes, Jesus was no rebel against his Jewish background. He was a faithful Jew; his distinctiveness was not in devising something new but in a full developing of what he had learned as a child and youth. How then can we fail to feel for the mother of Jesus a deep reverence and gratitude for all that she (with her husband Joseph) must have done for her son? Such reverence is a significant element in the devotion which the Christian tradition in its Catholic form has been ready to give her.

So far our focus has been on the so-called 'theological virtues' of faith, hope and love as manifested in Mary. What about the 'cardinal' virtues of prudence, temperance, fortitude and justice, taken into the Christian tradition from Greek thought and developed in the writings of Christian thinkers like Augustine and Thomas Aquinas? The basic reality of those 'cardinal virtues' was not unknown in Jewish thought, although of course they were not defined nor articulated in Greek fashion. A faithful Jew was supposed to be prudent in attitude and behaviour, rightly judging the ordering of things and living with a deep concern for such an ordering of existence. So also a faithful Jew would be temperate; indeed much of prophetic teaching is plainly directed against excess in food and drink and conduct. A loyal member of the Jewish community was to be a person of modest and restrained indulgence in the good things of this world. A devout Jew would also show fortitude or courage, both in defence of the Jewish tradition which had been handed down through the many centuries of Israel's past history, and also in preserving what was accepted in contemporary Jewish thought as right and true and good. And finally, a faithful Jew was expected to be a person who sought justice, lived righteously according to the requirements of the Torah and its interpretation, acted justly with those who were associated with him or her, and summed all this up by 'seeking God's kingdom and God's righteousness' – as Jesus himself is said to have phrased it.

As a faithful and devoted Jewess, Mary would have exhibited these same qualities, even though the place of women in Jewish society at the time would not make that expression so obvious in a woman as would be possible for a male – and here again we may mention Joseph's role as a father figure. Certainly in his being brought up in a loyal Jewish family, Jesus must have imbibed these qualities; and as he did so it must have been to a large degree through the influence upon him of his parents, not least of his mother.

To speak of Mary as model for all Christian discipleship does not imply that she took towards her son the attitude of commitment and dedication which is central in developed Christian faith. After all, that development did not occur until after Jesus' death and his 'rising again', even though there were intimations of some such belief in 'the days of his flesh'. He certainly awakened trust in himself, a sense of dependence upon him, and may even have made a claim to a place in God's purposes which could lead eventually to the belief that his was the human existence in which God had acted in a signal and decisive fashion. What can be said confidently is that in showing, by whatever she did or said, that she was a woman of faith, hope and love, and that she also possessed the qualities of prudence, temperance, fortitude and justice or righteousness which were appropriate to a devout Jewess, the mother of Jesus may indeed be seen as an example to all those who are prepared to call themselves Christians.

Besides what has already been said, we should notice that Mary was taken to be obedient to her calling. In the story of the annunciation she is represented as saying that she was 'the handmaid of the Lord' and that to God's will she would be obedient. Thus she is portrayed as receptive to the divine purpose so far as she was enabled to understand it. The later myths about her make this claim on her behalf. There is no reason to doubt that such a claim rests back upon some remembrance in the days of the very primitive Christian fellowship that she was precisely that sort of devout person.

Receptivity to God – or otherwise phrased, response to God as known in prayers and in participation in the life and beliefs of the Jewish community of faith – was no slight matter. To be able to say 'yes' to divine calling, so far as that can be understood, is the mark of the genuinely religious person. *A fortiori* it is the mark of the professing Christian. In this respect Mary stands before us as model. Thus she is to be imitated by those who participate in the church whose originative event is the existence of Mary's son. Our response is to be a fully conscious one to God in Christ; her response was to the God of Israel, along with obedience to what she took to be that God's will.

Any event, however novel it may be, has its continuity with the past from which it inherits. That past, as Whitehead phrased it, is 'causally efficacious in the present', providing both the background of and the possibilities for selection. At the same time there is novelty, with new lures and attractions which largely determine how the past will be used towards a future aim or goal. At the same time, every event has its 'relativity' – to a greater or lesser degree it is a 'creature of its own time and place'. For we do not have access to abstract and absolute truth which is lacking in continuity with its past and in associations in the present. This is significant when we see that Mary is a part of the total originating event of Christian faith, Jesus Christ.

In a profound sense we may say that she represented the continuity in what Jesus was and did with the whole Jewish heritage and its manifold expressions. These provided him with the milieu in which he lived and moved and had his being. At the same time, as a Jewish young woman Mary represented the relativity inevitable for human existence. A genuine theism, in which God is the final point of reference, must see deity as actively engaged both in the continuity with the past and in the novelty of each new moment, as well as providing in some fashion the context which establishes relationships for each and every instance in the creative process. The mother of Jesus surely conveyed to her son the reality of Jewish piety or faith. But she was 'conditioned' by the very circumstances in which she was able to do precisely this. The novelty about the originative event of Jesus Christ is the newness of God's action in, through and by him; but its continuity with the past is also 'of God'. The existence of Jewish faith and worship and moral understanding provided the setting for the novelty – and in that Jewish background we believe that God was active, for Jesus did not appear as a 'bolt from the blue'. At the same time he did not simply present a repetition of what Judaism had become by the time he was born and grew up, accepted his vocation, taught and acted and gave his life for the fulfilment of what he believed to be that calling. There was a novelty about him, as there is about every event in the movement of history. And in this total picture, with its unity and its complexity, the figure of Mary has its place and part. Jesus had a mother; naturally she had to be a specific person, with a specific character and with specific attitudes and actions. That is true of each one of us. If we try to lift Jesus out of that wide context and Mary's place in the picture, we succeed only in de-historizing him; and to do that will render him irrelevant to our human situation – which is in history and nowhere else.

To think thus of Mary as model for Christian discipleship does not for a moment contradict the 'newness' which appeared when in later days the faith in her son grew to fullness. She was not, because she could not be, aware of that developed Christian faith. Inevitably and naturally she remained in her own time and place. Nonetheless her life can stand as a symbol of the way in which the whole Jewish tradition was part of the *praeparatio evangelii* – the making ready of, and the preparation needed for, the newness which was in Jesus. But Christians should not forget that the right way of seeing her son, in the event of which he is centre and of which she is an integral part, is to discern that *there* – and a Christian would say, with a decisive quality – we glimpse what God is always 'up to' in the world and hence also what is a divinely purposed possibility for every human existence. There is a 'onceness' here, to be sure. All events have specificity and speciality. But there is also a 'for all-ness'. This event illuminates our picture of the divine character and the way in which God is ceaselessly operative in the world. So Mary can represent for all of us, whether we are Christian or not, the proper response to God's movement towards us.

In the story about Mary at the cross, Jesus is made to say that his friend John is to see in her his mother, while she is to see in John her son. The story may or may not be historically grounded, although I think that behind it there may very well be some genuine historical reminiscence. But the theological point which it makes is clear enough; and the devotional consequences are clear enough too. All who respond to whatever of God they know, in whatever terms this may take place, are 'sons of Mary'. Why? Because all are in the position of a possible response to, a possible receptivity for and a possible openness to, the divine purpose; and Mary is the symbol of the way in which humans should properly make their answer to the divine prevenience or initiating action upon them.

A recent translation of the splendid Latin words which used to be said in Holy Week in the Roman Catholic liturgy – *ubi caritas et amor, ibi deus est* ('where love and care are found, there God is present') – has these lines:

> Let us recall that in our midst
> Dwells God's begotten Son,
> As members of his Body joined
> We are in him made one.

34

No race nor creed can love exclude
If honoured be God's Name;
Our brotherhood embraces all
Whose Father is the same.

For those who are indeed 'members of his Body' and hence have become 'one in him', Mary can most properly be seen as the mother of us all. But since in principle the entire human race, with every man and woman and child who belongs to it, shares ultimately in 'the brotherhood' proper to those who have one divine Father, the implication is that Mary may be taken as the 'Mother-figure' for everyone. She shares with every member of the human race the opportunity to open self so that Christ may be born anew in each man and woman. That is a theme which must be discussed in more detail in the following chapter. For the moment we need only say that part of the splendour of the myth of Mary, with its historical setting in what little we know of her in direct factual data, is the way in which such a recognition of her place enriches our common human existence.

In a well-known hymn Charles Wesley asked for 'a heart to praise (his) God'; and in the same hymn he sketches the characteristics which will show that such a 'heart' has been granted. These include 'a heart, resigned, submissive, meek'; a heart which is 'humble, lowly, contrite'; a heart 'believing, true and clean', such that 'neither life nor death can part' it from the God whom it knows, 'full of love divine'. In fact, it will be a heart 'perfect, and right, and pure, and good' which will be a 'copy' of Christ's own heart and will have written upon it God's 'new, blest name of Love'. That hymn certainly is a description of what Christian discipleship is all about.

Am I indulging in absurdity when I note that there is a deep sense in which exactly such discipleship (granted the specific Christian conviction that its full realization is possible only when there is a vital sustained relationship with God disclosed in Mary's son as sheer Love) can be discerned in what we have been saying about the mother of the Lord? Obviously she did not have the privilege of a fully developed faith in her son, such as is now possible for those who have been grasped by the 'letting loose' through him of God's love into the world. Yet the picture of her which (from our slight historical data and from the developed myth about her significance) we can imaginatively take to have been the case is very close to the description Wesley gives in his hymn.

In the Christian tradition Mary has been taken as one who is indeed full of praise for God – the God of Israel whom she knew. And because of her faithfulness, hopefulness and love she has been seen also as resigned, submissive, meek in heart, humble, lowly in manner, contrite for her mistakes and deficiencies (whatever these may have been), believing, true and clean. She has been regarded as responding to the divine love as she was aware of it from the Judaism which was hers. She is taken to have been full of 'love divine'; with a perfection, rightness and purity that represent humankind at its best in and under whatever conditions were hers. It is appropriate therefore that she should be seen as model for genuine Christian discipleship, whatever else we may wish to say about that discipleship once her son is accepted as Lord.

4

Type of the Church and of a Redeemed World

During the past two or three decades I have written and published a number of essays, and in particular a book called *The Christian Church as Social Process* (1971), in all of which I have urged that our best way of understanding the Christian community of faith, worship and life is to see it as what in that book I called (as the title indicated) 'a social process'.

By this phrase I was emphasizing the organic and historical nature of the Christian community, using for the purpose some insights of Process thought. The point may be put in more traditional language by speaking of the church as a living tradition whose originating event was in Palestine two thousand years ago; which has continued down the centuries with its central faith inextricably associated with its ways of worship and life; and all three of these integrated or inter-related with one another. Its specific identity is established in its aim, which is the proclamation to (and acceptance by) men and women of the signal importance of Jesus Christ and what through him God has accomplished in the realm of human life – the bringing into existence of just such a community where the originating event is continually 'remembered' in the most profound and serious sense and where its release of the love of God has been renewed and experienced continually, with a response through a corporate life marked by the Spirit of Christ.

Such an approach to the meaning of the church is historically grounded; it makes sense of Christian experience; and it is in accordance with a more general conceptuality where the 'processive' nature of the world, and of its constituent events or happenings, is stressed. If we once grasp what is going on in the created order, then to think of the church in this fashion is illuminating in many and various ways that I need not spell out – save to say that one thing which clearly emerges is that the Christian community is not an 'organization' or 'institution' like so many good and valuable ones today, such as 'service clubs', groups brought together for social purposes and similar valuable human societies. The church's significance is deeper than any such groups; and in a remarkable way it is tied in with the event of Jesus Christ and whatever that event reveals of how God worked in the world.

As the community whose members (in different ways and with different intensity) have been grasped by the release of God's power in the acceptance, love and forgiveness given through the primary event of Jesus Christ, the Christian community is a community of response. Its members have been knit together in a fellowship which gives their lives new dignity, new perspective, new meaning and new power to live together in mutual concern. And this community finds its distinctive mode of expression in its acts of worship, chiefly in the celebration of the eucharist as the 'continual remembrance' of Christ, while its very existence strengthens its members to open their lives to God. Thus God's purpose of amorization, or increase in the range and strength of love, has in that community an instrument or agency in the realm of human affairs, where commitment to God defined in Jesus Christ leads to a devotion whose main manifestation is in the worship and prayer which empowers further action in the world.

Thus a deepened relationship to God is sought after and

in some degree attained, while at the same time there is an imperative such as will bring about renewed effort to carry out what is taken to be God's will – concerned as that will is with the spreading of love, which entails also a seeking for justice for all God's children so that they may be delivered from every sort of oppression (racial, economic, political, sexual) and freed to realize their human possibility. This 'life in grace' is established as redemption or salvation, 'fullness of life' or *shalom* (as the Hebrew puts it). In Pauline language, men and women are thus enabled to live 'in Christ'. Or, in the words used by St Benedict in the early days of the church, each of them is to be an 'other Christ', not in their own strength but by the continuing strength found in the Spirit released in the originative event.

Thus, Christianity is essentially a *life* and not a set of theological propositions, although these will inevitably emerge when men and women seek – as humans must always seek – to order in a coherent and consistent fashion what they have known in their concrete experience of living.

In accepting such interpretation of the Christian community we can understand how Mary has come to be regarded as a 'type of the church'.

Any placing of Mary in the context of Christian thought depends upon her 'belonging' to the church. Obviously that cannot mean that she had the developed beliefs which are characteristic of the community, nor that she took part in its developed worship. Nevertheless, as we are told, in the passage from Acts cited in our first chapter, in the days after the resurrection of her son she 'continued' in the fellowship of those who had been the first disciples. If this statement has historical validity – and of that we need have no doubt since there can have been no other reason for mentioning it – the mother of Jesus came early to Christian allegiance and was a member of the Christian fellowship in its primitive period.

What happened to her afterwards we do not know. Obviously she must have died, since this is the lot of all mortals. She may have died in great sanctity, as the early myth about her asserts. As the one who was known to be the mother of the risen Lord of the church, doubtless she died honoured by her companions in that community. Later theological speculation, building upon such a likelihood, was prepared to argue that she was 'assumed' into heaven – that is, taken into God – in a fashion which eventually led to extravagant doctrinal statements. Yet all the way through, there was never any doubt that she belonged with the Christian company, so that in the course of time she could well be called 'the mother of all Christians' and could be taken as what I have styled 'a type' of the church in its corporate response to God manifested in her son, by whose Spirit the church existed and for whose continuing work in the world it served.

In the preceding chapter we have spoken of Mary as model for Christian discipleship. She has been portrayed as one whose life was marked by faithfulness, by hopeful expectation of God's will being done in the world, by love and concern, by obedience to the vocation which she took to be hers. Precisely such qualities are intended to mark the personal and corporate Christian life. Hence we can see readily how she came to be regarded as a model or a 'type' for the church itself.

In the Eastern Orthodox churches mariological 'dogmatic definition' has not been so strongly developed as in the Western world, although in those churches we often find what E. L. Mascall has styled an 'exuberant and flamboyant expression' of mariological devotion, not least in the liturgy but also in a good deal of popular piety. This reverence for Mary is implied in much else that is said by the Orthodox; and the names given her in Orthodoxy are as exalted as those found in the Western Christian world.

In the popular piety of the Orthodox and Roman Catholic church we are aware of what might be described as a sense of intimacy with the mother of Jesus, coupled with a remarkable tenderness of spirit. In terms of official theology, Mary's relationship to the church as the body of Christ has been stated in the last part of Vatican II's *Dogmatic Constitution on the Church*. In that document, which is a considerable modification of position from extreme ultramonatism and post-Tridentine teaching, there is a concluding chapter especially devoted to the subject. The more traditional bishops at that council wished to give her an entirely independent treatment, but by a majority (said not to have been very large) of those present at Vatican II it was decided that Mary should be included in the discussion of the church itself. The result of that decision, as shown in the document which was finally adopted, was to speak of Mary in the context of a wider ecclesiology or discussion of the nature and function of the church. Whatever is to be said about her must in no way be a 'derogation of, or addition to, the dignity and efficacy of Christ the one mediator'. Rather, everything said about her must be in closest relationship both with Christ himself and with the church's nature. In other words, Mary is to be represented as having her place as a genuine, yet also a subordinate, part of the total event of Jesus Christ. She is seen as a member of 'Christ's mystical body', in a fashion appropriate to one who had been 'chosen' by God to be the mother of Jesus. Like the rest of the church's membership, she is among those who have been 'redeemed' through her son in the originative event of Christian faith.

I have observed above that when Pope Paul VI promulgated this constitution of Vatican II he declared explicitly that Mary should be considered as 'Mother of the Church'. This is not a novel view; it rests back upon the very ancient interpretation of her as 'the second Eve', called this

41

because through her consenting role in the conception and birth of her son she was the instrumental means through which the first Eve's sin – as told in the Genesis story – was overcome, not of course in and by Mary herself, but by what God accomplished in her son.

Protestant Christians have rejected almost entirely the development of mariology, although in recent years some of them have been less negative about her. On the other hand, while Anglicanism has not made any formal theological statement on the matter there has always been a certain amount of mariological devotion in Anglican circles. This first took place during the seventeenth century, thanks to some of the Caroline divines; more recently, 'high churchmen' or Anglo-Catholics have often put considerable emphasis on mariological doctrine, although never of the perhaps exaggerated sort sometimes found in Roman Catholic circles.

What may be said today by those of us who with all our loyalty to the deep insights of the broad Catholic tradition of Christianity yet also feel it necessary to take a markedly different theological attitude, as well as (perhaps) to use another philosophical conceptuality as a context for Christian faith? What can *we* make of the notion that Mary is indeed a 'type of the church' and in some sense can be regarded both as a member of it and also as its 'mother'? Is all this simply nonsensical talk, alien to the true genius of Christian faith, or does it have a residual value such as I urged in the last chapter?

It will be obvious that my own view is in accordance with the latter possibility. However much we may wish to re-conceive or re-work our inherited theology, those of us who are convinced that in some profound way the Spirit of God has guided the living tradition cannot help feeling that there is something here (as in the other aspects of mariological discourse) of which we must take account and for which we must find a place in contemporary Christian thinking and devotion.

Precisely how this is to be done is another matter. In this book I have been seeking to suggest a 'how' which is aware of modern biblical scholarship, is in accordance with the experiential reality of life within the community, and is prepared to grant (even to insist) that often material which is mythological in nature is not simply to be dismissed as irrelevant or unimportant but rather is to be seen (precisely in its mythological quality) as telling us significant things that are found in dedicated allegiance to the basic affirmations of Christian faith, worship and discipleship. Undoubtedly this requires a different sort of statement in respect to the 'person and work of Jesus'; but equally certainly we can turn to consideration of the long history of devotion to the mother of Jesus herself – who is always to be seen as part of the total event we indicate when we speak of Jesus of Nazareth as 'Lord and Christ'.

Hence I propose that in our establishing the identity of the living tradition or 'social process' which is the church, Mary had a role to play. Even John Calvin (as I noted earlier) was ready to allow this; although of course he rejected altogether doctrinal and devotional 'excesses', as doubtless he would have called them even if he did not think of them as sheer error.

To repeat what has been said several times already, it is undeniable that Jesus had a mother and that this mother was the one whose response made possible not only his birth into the world but also the way in which he came later to understand and accept his vocation and to set about fulfilling it in accordance with what he conceived to be the will of his 'father in heaven'. To speak in that fashion is only to talk common sense. When we go beyond that we are building upon the fruitfulness which we believe has been found in the developing veneration accorded to his mother.

No doubt some will deny that there is any such fruitfulness. But those of us who have been brought up with, and have found enhancement of Christian discipleship through a sincere veneration for Mary, must take another line.

For us the kind of Christian spirituality which follows from that positive acceptance of the tradition seems lovely, gracious and compelling. It is the sort of piety which led such a non-Christian as E. M. Forster to find the Latin expression of Christianity attractive in a way which he did not find in the variety of Christianity which he had known as a young man in typical English 'evangelical' piety. There was a warmth, a colour and a deep humanism in Latin Christianity which for him was preferable to the austerity and aridity that he had previously experienced. As one who knew him well, I rather suspect that it was the aridity and austerity, even more than the apparent 'incredibility', of 'poor little Christianity' (as he once called it), which led him to a sceptical, indeed agnostic, attitude towards the Christian enterprise as a whole. To Forster it seemed barren, unaesthetic and so stringently moralistic in tone that it was repressive of all that can make human existence appealing, interesting and attractive. Call this Forster's 'rationalization', if you will. For my part, I am sure that this was the case.

I have spoken earlier about the complexity and yet the unity of each event in the cosmic process. This provides a clue to the approach which, as it seems to me, can enable us to give a genuine place to Mary and discover meaning in talk about marian devotion. It also helps to make sense of her being both model for personal Christian discipleship and also a type of the church's nature as responsive to God's activity in the primary Christian event. She is indeed part of the event, as I have urged; without her it could not have taken place as it did, although obviously it might have taken place in some other fashion. But what Christian insight has seen in the role of Mary cannot be dismissed simply as a matter of pleasant legendary talk or a variety of fanciful pious discourse. Because it *is* integral to the total event no such easy dismissal is possible. Throughout this book I have urged that respect for the living tradition is an essential element in our discipleship as members of the Christian community. Of course this does not imply that we are credulously to accept anything and everything that has turned up in that tradition's development of devotion and thought. We need to be critical as well as loyal. But we can readily be both and I hope that what I have been urging so far *is* both.

The title of this chapter speaks of Mary as a type both of the church and of the world understood as redeemed by God. To the latter aspect of the topic we must now turn.

In some discussions of Christianity a great separation has been made between the Christian community's life, devotion and thought, on the one hand, and the created world as seen both in history and in the order of nature, on the other. In such discussions the two seem to have no relationship one with the other; we have a kind of ecclesiocentric view which appears to reject altogether God's wider range of activity. Or conversely, we have a view which is so focussed on history and nature that the Christian community's existence and the insights which it conveys may be regarded as ultimately irrelevant. In terms of our present topic, the consequence of this dichotomy may be the idea that what is said about Mary has no reference whatsoever to what is going on in the world at large but is an entirely 'self-contained' Christian prejudice. Or, on the other hand, it may lead to a refusal to find anything important in that mariological tradition. In that case, talk about mariological matters becomes Christian 'in-talk' without genuine value, to be dismissed as jargon associated with a narrow kind of belief, popular with people who do not live in the 'real world'.

But any such total separation is unnecessary; indeed, it is

45

also disloyal to the way in which, as a matter of actual fact, the church has always been 'in the world'; and yet in the world with a message that invokes something that is not merely human nor natural but speaks of God and the divine action in the whole creation. For the church is part of that creation. The corollary of this is that the world in its widest historical and natural order is the inevitable context for the Christian community. What is said about the latter has its relevance to what we may wish to say about the former.

An important aspect of the Christian use of the process conceptuality is its recognition of this intimate relationship. No event can be properly understood save in that wider context. We might put this by saying epigrammatically that an event has meaning only in an 'eventful' world. Its implications are of great importance when we are attempting to understand the Christian community as itself an event which like all events must be seen as conforming to the pattern whose general principles, despite particular differences, run through the entire creation.

I have urged that the church is a 'social process'. It had its beginnings in specific occurrences, centrally in what happened in and around Jesus of Nazareth. Yet it was not exhausted in that originative event; it has its 'ongoing' reality. It would be a mistake to attempt to confine its full reality to the originative event. We cannot confine our attention in any adequate grasp of things only to one particular historical moment, even to the origination one.

Some of my fellow Process thinkers have criticized me because I have argued that the deepest significance of Jesus can only be properly grasped when we take into account what Whitehead called 'the stream of influence' which proceeded from his existence in history. My critics have said that we should interpret Jesus in the light of the immediacy of the concrete moment in history during which he lived among us as a man. But I am sure that this would confine the event, and to my mind confine it illegitimately, to that time and place 'when and where Jesus lived'. On the contrary, I urge that what has happened afterwards in consequence of that given moment is not only important but is essential for us to emphasize if we are to come to any adequate evaluation of 'who Jesus was' and 'what Jesus did'.

This is only another way of saying that the existence of the Christian community is integral to the event and that Jesus is always to be understood in and with those who have been affected and influenced by him down the ages, even to our own day. The originative event is in some genuine fashion continued in succeeding ages by the responsive community we call the church; and the church itself (as a continuing 'social' event) is to be seen as having a part and place in the wider process of the world. Here we have a clue to why the belief that Mary is the type not only of the church but also of the redeemed world is both relevant and valuable.

What has gone on in the complex event of Jesus Christ is indeed indicative of what goes on in the world at large. When and as the world, the totality of the created order, responds properly to the divine will and purpose and to the unfailing activity of God in and upon it, that created order is the place for the fulfilment of what in the Christian fellowship is present as an *arrabon* or first-fruits. If this is true, then Mary is quite appropriately described as the type of what the world is to become.

Finally and briefly, the eucharist – which is the central and definite mark of the Christian church – is a preliminary manifestation of this redeemed creation. It too is an action; it too is inescapably part of the total Christian event. Thus it is entirely right that in the course of the eucharistic action reference is to be made (however modestly and indirectly) to Mary. She is among those included in 'the whole company of heaven' who with 'angels and archangels' are united with living Christian people in the offering of the 'sacrifice of praise and thanksgiving' which the Christian fellowship delights to carry on day by day, week by week, as it unfailingly 'remembers', and hence makes still present, the enactment of God in the man Jesus.

With this we must also and necessarily associate the prayers of all those who are 'members of Christ'. We must associate ourselves in their work in carrying on the purposes of God defined in Christ. The whole Christian enterprise is knit together in a unity of faith, worship and life. Within it Mary is honoured and revered. It is right to offer her our veneration without in any way thinking to exalt her to divinity. Some humans are to be accorded special recognition; and in her case, the recognition rests back upon her being the one who conceived and bore the Lord through whom for us God is known and worshipped in a distinctive manner. So she is 'blessed among women', blessed because those who have responded to the figure central in the Christian event must say first of all that 'blessed is the fruit of [her] womb, Jesus'.

5

Devotion to Mary

Several years ago I wrote an essay for a British religious periodical in which I sought to present not a defence for, but an explanation of, the practice by Catholics in Latin countries, especially in Italy, of addressing prayers to St Mary. In that article I pointed out that the dominant religious teaching in those countries has portrayed 'God the Father' as so transcendent and remote that it is difficult for ordinary people to think that this God could be reached by their prayer. Furthermore, I noted that the implicit christology of much said in such countries makes Jesus Christ so much divine that his humanity receives little if any emphasis. Hence he too seems largely 'unavailable' for prayer. Finally, in many so-called 'Catholic' lands, I observed that popular teaching about the Holy Spirit has tended to identify that Spirit almost exclusively with specifically ecclesiastical concerns and actions. Thus the Spirit seems not to be 'at hand' for the ordinary praying man or woman or child.

But men and women and children in those countries do wish to engage in prayer; and they do hope that in prayer they may be in touch with a divine reality that is 'genuinely adorable and 'at hand'. For a large number of Latin Catholics Mary seems to be very much on the 'divine side', so far as their thinking goes; yet she is also regarded as truly human and hence as available, loving, merciful and gracious to her fellow humans. Thus Mary becomes for them a vivid and vital human symbol of 'whatever-is-divine' and she can be addressed confidently and hopefully because, as human, she understands what it is like to be human.

In concluding that essay I ventured to make this comment: 'The divine Post Office is much more efficiently organized than the British Post Office; and prayers addressed to St Mary, or indeed to any of the saints, are immediately forwarded to "the throne of Grace" and are gladly received by God.' In other words, I was suggesting that the God who loves and cares for us men and women (who are made in the divine image, however battered that image may now be because of human sin), is the one and only true God who responds to any and every heartfelt prayer, no matter how imperfect may be the address 'on the envelope'.

A few days later I received a letter from a prominent bishop who himself was well known as being a leader on the 'evangelical' side of the Church of England. He thanked me for the article, which (he said) was the first account he had ever read in which a meaningful answer was given to what had always been for him a serious question when he travelled in Mediterranean lands: 'Why do so many people there pray to St Mary and not immediately to God? and what possible sense can such praying make?'

I recount this unimportant incident because it provides an introduction to the subject in this chapter, which is the significance and place of mariological devotion in the living Christian tradition. Of course I do not commend the substitution of petitions or intercessions addressed to St Mary for prayers to God. But I do want to make a responsible case for what in this book I am calling 'a chastened devotion' towards the mother of Jesus.

I admit that very often this devotion has been anything but 'chastened'; often it has been greatly exaggerated and on occasion it can seem highly superstitious. Yet it may very well be true, and I believe that it is true, that veneration for the mother of our Lord is appropriate and proper and that it does not at all negate the deep conviction of sound theology that it is to God and to God only that *latreia* is to be directed.

That great word *latreia* means 'worship'; and in classical theology it has always been distinguished both from *dulia*, which is defined as the reverence due to any of God's creatures but especially to humans, and from *hyperdulia* or a specially intensive sort of reverence which can be felt for St Mary. This distinction is found in St Thomas Aquinas, who urges that only to God is full worship (*latreia*) to be given. But at the same time he urges that we are to reverence (*dulia* is named) all men and women as 'made in God's image'; while to St Mary he says that it is licit and right to offer *hyperdulia* or a high degree of veneration or devotion precisely because she is the mother of Jesus the incarnate Son of God.

Some groups of Christians have refused any sort of reverence or veneration or devotion to Mary. Sometimes they have even been inclined to say that no human being deserves reverence, because all humans are sinful, alienated from the divine reality and disobedient to the divine will. That is the extreme Protestant position. But in the Catholic tradition, however, a very different view has been taken. That tradition has insisted that every human being is deserving of a respect which in practice amounts to reverence, since every human being is a 'creature of God' and 'in God's image'; and since in every human there remains (despite the presence of sin), a genuine trace of divine reality. Furthermore, in principle, if not always in fact all humans are capable of some genuine response to God's loving movement towards them. That same Catholic tradition, in both its Eastern and Western forms, has been ready to go on to say that the mother of Jesus, precisely because she was sufficiently 'engraced' as his human mother, is not indeed raised out of genuine human existence but nevertheless represents that existence when it is rightly fulfilling its proper function. Thus she was God's 'hand-maiden', through whom God had acted and by whose consent the coming of Jesus was made possible.

In addition, it is worth noticing that in the Eastern Orthodox churches there is also a willingness to permit, even to encourage, prayers which are addressed to any persons who have departed this life. I shall refer again to this practice in our final chapter; but here it may be said that there is a natural and readily understandable reason for this Orthodox custom.

If it is proper for me to ask someone whom I know here and now, perhaps particularly a person whom I love and who loves me, for her or him to give help or guidance or indeed a gift of any sort, it is difficult to see why I should not continue doing this when that person is no longer present with me in this world. However we may wish to interpret the 'communion of saints', we humans are surely bound together in a community inclusive of all humankind living or dead. We rely on and are dependent upon one another. None of us lives in and of and to himself or herself. To be sure, bodily death is the end of our present mortal existence and we do not know what is beyond death – most of the portrayals of the state 'after death' are at best imperfect, and probably they may be highly erroneous. Yet we do know, if we are Christians at all, that somehow the departed are within God's life – 'we cannot drift beyond his love and care', as the hymn puts it.

We have every Christian reason to be confident that God treasures those persons and their achievements, as God also uses them for the furthering of the divine purposes of love. It seems entirely legitimate to think that God also values our remembrance of them. In the mystery of the divine life and purpose God must then value also our asking them to help us in our earthly existence. As I suggested in respect to the prayers of believers in Latin lands, who pray to the mother of Jesus, these prayers too may be 'forwarded on' to God who understands our human ignorance and our human interdependence, as well as our wish to continue in a loving relationship with all 'whom we have loved and lost awhile'. Such praying is an expression of that relationship, often made in anguish but often too in delight; and surely God understands and rejoices in the 'comfort' or strengthening which can follow from just such an address to dear ones no longer at our side.

It is in this context, I think, that we can best come to see what is involved in a devotion to Mary, especially when that devotion has led God's children to speak to her in their praying. But this is by no means the whole of the veneration which the Catholic tradition would wish to accord to the mother of Jesus.

When I say that we are also urged to love St Mary and to think of her as 'Our Lady', some will doubtless regard this as a very sentimental, even a mistaken, way of speaking. How can we love one about whom our historical information is so slight? How can we love one who has been made the subject of legendary narrative and about whom there has grown up so much that I have acknowledged to be 'myth'? My answer at this point is first to quote lines from a hymn which is sung in some Roman and Anglican parishes. 'How should we not love thee, Mother dear, whom Jesus loved so well?' As I have argued earlier, devotion to Mary is intimately tied in with devotion to Jesus Christ – and not only to Jesus as in some sense an 'act of God' but to Jesus as human or as a man.

There is a devotion in many Catholic circles to what is styled 'the sacred heart'. This devotion has frequently been phrased in an idiom which is almost crudely anatomical. Yet what its founders, blessed John Eudes and others, intended to teach was a devotion to Jesus in his true manhood. In reaction from an excessive stress on what is usually known as 'the divinity of Jesus', those pious and saintly Christians wished to urge that we need also to recognize and adore 'the humanity of Jesus'. The two – divinity and humanity – are so closely united that they bring before us two main emphases in Catholic Christian faith: God acts humanly, on the one hand, so that the human instrument or agent for the divine action is integrally one with God: on the other hand, Jesus' humanity is the humanity which he received from his mother. 'Like mother, like child': his is a humanity largely formed and nurtured by her. In that humanity which was his he could not have been what in fact he was, had it not been for the care and love of his mother. This is true for any one of us; it is a basic element in my human existence. How could it be otherwise with Jesus, if indeed he was truly human and not a demi-god or an eccentric intrusion from without (and where would that be?) into the realm of human existence and experience.

A few days before I wrote these words I had the privilege of a long meeting with a distinguished Australian child psychologist. During our conversation he was emphatic in stressing the inescapable role that a mother plays in the development of her child's character. Without the love of a mother, he was ready to insist, no child grows up to be a fully realized adult; otherwise there are bound to be distortions or inclinations which get in the way of and often can prevent really sound growth. I ventured to remark to my acquaintance that it seemed to me that a recognition of this truth in the case of Jesus and his mother was highly important in Christian thought and practice and could even be said to have its significant place in the attitude which we took to his mother. I was not surprised when he agreed with me and went on to stress the validity of the mariological aspect in the 'incarnation' of God in human life. Of course I was obliged to urge that it is not necessary for us always to use the conventional and traditionally-hallowed word 'incarnation' in our assertion of the focal and decisive importance of the event of Jesus Christ. But that was a side-issue; it did not in any way affect the main point which he was making and which I found so instructive.

Precisely because of the position of Mary as the mother of Jesus, the one who bore him, brought him up, taught him, cared for him, looked after his needs, and introduced him as a child to religious faith, she is worthy of our love. How could it possibly be otherwise?

But there is still more to be said in this connection. Any genuine devotion leads to imitation. Here we come once again to the point made in our third chapter about Mary as a model for all Christian discipleship – and because a model, one who is to be esteemed, respected, and loved for what she was and for what she did. We cannot accept a model and at the same time hate or despise what we have accepted. Somehow or other we must love it.

What has just been said does not derogate from the decisive importance of the event of Jesus Christ. It only points to an aspect of that event which has often been forgotten. Nor does it substitute a 'creature' for God. Even in the case of Jesus Christ, we may recall, classical theology has never accorded his humanity as such the *latreia* proper to God alone. To that humanity, it has said, is to be given what might be defined as the highest possible type of *hyperdulia*. Only when the Chalcedonian version of 'incarnation' (or the neo-Chalcedonian one which later was so generally accepted in theological circles), has been taken to mean that the 'self' of Jesus Christ was the divine Word or *Logos* which had 'taken' a human 'nature' that lacked any genuine human 'self' or (as in more informed discussion) 'subsumed' the human self to the divine self – only then could *latreia* or proper worship of Jesus' manhood be approved. This raises a difficult christological question, to which further and fuller reference will be made in the sixth chapter.

In the 'chastened' devotion to Mary that I am defending, there is love for her because of her vocation. We have seen that there is also veneration, an honouring of Mary as the mother of Jesus, as model for Christian discipleship, and as 'type' (so I have phrased it) of the Christian church as the Body of Christ, through which his Spirit is still at work in the world by human agents knit together in the Spirit-inspired fellowship.

I have urged that Mary symbolizes the obedience of a creature to the divine will and plan. The church too is thus to be obedient. It does not exist for itself nor for its own perpetuation or aggrandisement. Its whole meaning is found in its mission, which is the continuing doing for Christ of that which 'he began both to do and to teach' in the days when he walked the lanes of Palestine and when later he went to the cross in fulfilling his vocation as he had been brought to understand it. Furthermore, in the divine purpose the whole world is intended to be an instrument for God's loving activity. It does not exist for itself alone. In the ultimate sense its purpose is to be open to God's action upon it and in it. Being thus open to divine action, it is to be the sacramental means by which that action is to be carried out. Here (as so often) Eastern Orthodox Christians have something to teach the rest of us. Many of the thinkers in that tradition claim that the creation itself is to 'become the church'. The Christian community is taken to be a 'sacred and wonderful mystery', not only in its own particular vocation but also because it is 'the Body of Christ'. And like the church in its deepest reality, the world is to be God's 'body'. I may remark here that in some contemporary Process theologians a similar assertion may be found. Charles Hartshorne, for example, is prepared to say that the created order stands to God as the self stands to its body; here he is only echoing a phrase of Thomas Aquinas, doubtless without being aware of it. For Aquinas taught that an analogy may properly be drawn between God and creation, on the one hand, and what Aquinas calls 'the soul' and the human body, on the other.

Thus we have an interesting and illuminating sort of progression. As the human existence of Jesus Christ was the 'body' (not simply a physical organism but the totality of that human existence) of the God who through him acted in the event called by his name, so also the church stands to the 'whole Christ' as the 'body' for his purposes. And the world stands to God as his intended 'body' – with Jesus Christ as the supreme symbol or classical instance in the ongoing process.

Just here, the mother of Jesus also has her significance. She was the one who bore the humanity which was Jesus' own; and by extension she is the 'type' for the church as Christ's 'body' in a different but related sense. In this context she is also the 'type' of what the world in God's intention is to become, when all things are brought into obedience to the divine will and way in creating and redeeming and making available new possibilities of fulfilment – and all as the expression of God's unfailing love.

Once again, if the figure of Mary as presented in the historical data and in the reading of her significance in the later-developed 'myth' can be seen to represent the 'virtues' which are integral to genuinely faithful and obedient human life, she can be seen as proper for our devotion. About those 'virtues' I have already spoken in another chapter; here I need only note once again that I am talking about the 'habits', as the scholastic theologians described them, which are the right and divinely-purposed mode of human behaviour, that bring men and women to their proper fulfilment precisely as human.

In ways like those sketched in the last few pages, we may well see that the mother of Jesus, while she was an 'ordinary woman' in one sense, was in another sense 'special'. For after all, Jesus could have had only one mother; and in that sense she can certainly be called special – as indeed can every event (human or natural) in the world process. Again, as the 'consenting cause' of the event of Jesus Christ, through her ready response to divine calling, she was 'special' and has the more claim to our veneration.

I end this chapter by some comments on the fruitfulness in Christian life which follows from thus honouring the mother of Jesus.

One point suggests itself immediately. Obviously a good deal of profound Christian piety is found in those Protestant groups which fail to accord to Mary any sort of devotion. Yet sometimes this piety can be arid. Not only is it often all too masculine, like the God about whom it seems to speak. That would be bad enough, some of us are bound to say. But what is also often lacking in the worship found in such groups is any feeling of genuine warmth. Indeed the bareness of their meeting-places is often evidence of this chilling sort of worship. There is also and frequently a tendency to reject any use of bodily expression in worship, as part of what seems a determined refusal to appeal to the sensuous aspect of human life – to our human 'feeling-tones. On the contrary, the traditions which allow a devotion to Mary seem also to allow, indeed to demand, a more full-bodied kind of worship. Probably this is associated with the insistence in those traditions on the importance of what is stereotypically called the 'feminine' side of life. To be sure, the familiar 'masculine-feminine' contrast will not stand up to careful examination. Many males have deep 'feminine' qualities and many females have deep 'masculine' qualities; a completely realized human life ideally should have both in a proper balance. Nonetheless, it remains true that Catholic worship, like Catholic piety, has warmth, colour and a vivid appeal to the senses, which make it attractive to many of us – perhaps to more people than we often think, and especially to those whose existence may have been starved and impoverished in a world like ours today.

A certain remarkable beauty is found in the figure of Mary as she has been portrayed in great art. Statues which show her with the baby in her arms, moving representation of her sorrow in such works of art as Michelangelo's *Pietà*, and much else in painting and sculpture speak with enormous effect. We cannot dismiss such matters. Beauty of all sorts is one of the channels through which God speaks to humankind. The divine communication is not to be confined to verbal symbols, but includes the plastic, dramatic, colourful and harmonious symbolizing of which all great art (not *kitsch* of course) is the manifestation. Some people are inclined to urge that the 'aesthetic' aspect in experience is secondary to the rational, logical, ethical and volitional in that experience. However, to neglect the 'aesthetic' would seem to imply a very inadequate conception of the working of the divine in our human experience. And I should myself wish to urge that great religion, religion at its best, is much more an aesthetic reality than it is a rational or even a moral reality, significant and necessary as these latter may be.

Hence I am prepared to say that one of the reasons for a veneration of Mary, yet without exaggerations or indulgence in sheer fantasy, is simply that such devotion produces, as it also expresses, something of genuine beauty in our human living. Why should we be afraid of it? Probably such fear is an expression of an inhuman unwillingness to concede that God is indeed to be seen as a 'beauty ever old, yet ever new', to use St Augustine's fine words. God is 'lovely' in both senses of that word. That is, God is loving (and indeed Love) and God is alluring and attractive. God is the *summum bonum*, the summation and completion of all the partial goods known in the world – and *bonum* here is not so much moral perfection, although of course it is that, as it is the satisfaction of right human desiring and the full actualization of the harmonious of which (even in this finite world) we have hints and intimations.

To many of us the figure of Mary as the mother of Jesus is beautiful; it is lovely. That suggests in another way that she is one whom we may venerate and for whom we may entertain a true devotion. For many centuries, millions of devout Christian people have found here much help in devotional practices which (while like all good things open to abuse) have proved a means of human enrichment.

To take a few examples of this we may refer specifically to the use of the 'rosary', to the salutation 'Hail Mary', and to the 'Angelus' said at several times during the day. In Eastern circles, mariological veneration has often been more directly associated with the divine liturgy, the eucharist, and other church services. In the West, however, the personal use of the three devotions just mentioned has been commonly accepted as valuable. Since Vatican II many Roman Catholics have probably tended more to follow the Eastern Orthodox usage. But with slight modifications (perhaps made largely for theological reasons to be noted in our sixth chapter), those popular ways of honouring the mother of Jesus can very well be used by any Christian. Indeed some recent books by Anglican Evangelicals and English Methodists have urged exactly this. But whether these 'devotions' are used or not used the main point stands firm. 'Chastened' devotion to Mary is both a legitimate and a helpful aspect of Christian piety – all of which, in the long run, is ultimately directed towards God. For what Aquinas said of the theology of Christian eucharistic prayer is true of *all* Christian praying: it is *to* God the father, *through* God defined because he has been disclosed to us in the event of Jesus Christ and with St Mary as an integral part of that event, and *in* the Holy Spirit who enables the response of men and women to the action of God towards them and in them.

6

Mary and God-in-Christ

Hence relevance to wide sweep of theology

My insistence that the mother of Jesus is integrally related to, is indeed part of, the total event of Jesus Christ can be put in terms of traditional Christian theology by saying that discussion of mariological matters belongs essentially with the discussion of christological matters. In other words, what we say about her will necessarily be associated with what we say about her son – *she* was *his* mother.

It has always been the conviction of the ongoing tradition which is the Christian community that the event of Jesus Christ is properly understood only when it is seen as part of the wide and general activity of God in human history, an activity which not only discloses God's nature and God's ways of working in the world but also effects the release in that world of divine grace – the energy of divine love – to the sons and daughters of God. The basic issue in all theology is the character of God, how God may be pictured, and how we may best come to understand what God is 'up to' in the world at large. Or more simply put, theology's concern is the right way we humans can 'describe God', once we take Jesus Christ (in the complexity yet unity of the event of which he is the centre) as our chief clue. It is here too that the figure of his mother has its part to play.

One of the difficulties with a good deal of conventional, and indeed of much traditional, christological discussion has been the adoption of wrong 'models'. In earlier writing on this subject I have indicated why I believe this to be the case; and I may refer here especially to my discussion in two

61

chapters found in *Catholic Faith in a Process Perspective* (1981) and in *Picturing God* (1982), where I have put my position in fairly brief form. Here is a summary of my arguments.

If we think of God in Christ as a union of two 'substances' divine and human, we are bound to emphasize either the divine or the human in such a way that the other member of the pair receives less than adequate attention. If we think in terms of 'wills', divine and human, then we do the same thing – stress one to the minimizing of the other. If our model is two 'consciousnesses', one divine and the other human, once again we shall put our emphasis on one partner in such a fashion that the other will not be stressed. And in the history of thought about christology we find that exactly such one-sidedness has taken place. Jesus is regarded as essentially divine and only adjectively human. Or in relation to that position, he is essentially human and only adjectively divine. This is how the discussion has been carried on.

For many of us today it seems more accurate to say that in the event of Jesus Christ – including in that event all that prepared for his coming, the data which we possess about his historical existence, the way in which he was 'received' or rejected, and the 'stream of influence' which has proceeded from him – we have an instance of genuine and full humanity. Jesus was human in every sense of the word. But at the same time, Christian faith has correctly discerned in that humanity a divine working or activity, and hence a genuine presentness of God, such that Jesus must be given a distinctive and decisive place by those who have thus been drawn into his total impact. And it is precisely in the total event, with what I have called all its complexity and all its unity, that the figure of Mary has its proper place. She is inescapably part of the total event, that is to say, Jesus had a mother like all humans but the mother whom he had was this one and no other. The significance of that brief statement will be noted in the sequel.

When the event of Jesus Christ is taken as profoundly indicative both of God's character or nature and of God's mode of actions in the creation, certain inescapable conclusions follow about what God *is*. Just here much generally accepted theology, not to speak of much commonly accepted spirituality and worship, has failed to give attention to the implications of that central fact. God has often been seen as remote first cause or as abstract metaphysical principle, or as like an oriental tyrant or like a moral dictator. In such theology God has not been seen as nothing but 'pure unbounded love', such as was humanly enacted in Jesus. This failure has inevitably had its affect on how Jesus Christ himself is interpreted. For only when and as love is given its supreme place in the picture can we hope to arrive at an adequate christology. And here too what we say about Mary, Jesus' mother, is intimately part of the picture.

The basic Christian affirmation is that through what I have styled the total event of Jesus Christ, as this has been communicated to man and woman in the Christian community of faith, God is disclosed and released as sheer Love-in-act. Of course such a proclamation cannot be demonstrated from an uncommitted scientific inspection of the historical material we possess in the Gospels and elsewhere in the New Testament. Nonetheless, precisely such a way of picturing God as Love-in-act has as a matter of fact been derived from what happened in and around Jesus of Nazareth; nothing in the material we do possess is incongruous with that proclamation while much in it (if not everything) can be read as affirming it in one way or another. Since this is true, our best clue for the working-out of a doctrine of Christ – who he was in terms of what he did – will be through the use of this received 'model' of God as Love-in-act. Why? Because this 'model' serves us better than the models of substance or will or consciousness to which I

63

have just referred. This is because it can be used in a fashion that genuinely maintains the full integrity of Jesus' humanity, while at the same time it permits us to speak meaningfully of God's activity and hence God's presence in him.

This can be put quite simply by saying that in the event of Jesus Christ, as Christian faith has seen it and in consequence has sought to live by it, there has been found a coincidence of God's prevenient and initiating Love *and* a human response to it in obedience and dedication. The coincidence – call it 'union' if you wish – is not accidental nor incidental; for Christians it is an essential fact wrought out in history. Yet this does not mean that Jesus is taken as 'entirely alone', so to say, without any reference to the wider range of God's activity in the creation and above all in the realm of human affairs. On the contrary, it meets the requirements noted at the beginning of this chapter since it illuminates, makes sense of, and gives sense to, all that God is doing in the world. In other words, what is potential in the very fact of creation, what in various ways and in differing degrees is to be seen actualized in that creation, has had what I have styled a focal and decisive expression in what went on in and through Jesus of Nazareth. Christian faith discerns there both God's loving reach into human existence and also human existence in its loving response to that divine activity.

I have said that we must see the event of Christ as a total event; and as such it must include the mother of Jesus. She is neither an incidental nor accidental element in the story but integral to it by virtue of her having been the woman who both gave birth to and who loved and nurtured the one who is at the heart of the total event. What does that suggest to us?

One thing which is implicit here is that through granting to Mary her proper role in the event, we are also seeing how the inherited strongly paternal Hebrew conception of God is modified by the presence in it of a concern for maternal care and tenderness. The Jews had long thought of God as the creator of all things, the 'ruler' of the world, the final moral authority, the divine reality to be worshipped and obeyed – a basically masculine concept. In that Jewish tradition there were indeed strong intimations of divine caring and love, of God's *chesed* or 'faithful loving-mercy'. And this aspect of deity was given over the years a growing importance; and it had received specific stress in parts of the oracles of Isaiah, Jeremiah and Hosea, to mention three of the great Jewish prophets. Thus the concept of God as force or sheer power, as sovereign-ruler and as moral governor had been modified and there was a significant and profound recognition of what might be styled the 'feminine' aspect of deity. What the event of Christ in its fullness does is to give an added emphasis to the awareness of this 'feminine' in God. It brings that awareness to a point and places it in a central position when God is being talked about.

Hence what might have been a somewhat generalized view of God as Love was now given a vivid illustration. This is a highly important matter. For general truths however important 'cut no ice' unless and until they are shown in this or that particular instance. The event of Jesus Christ is for Christian faith *the* instance or – as I have often phrased it in my christological writings mentioned above – that event with the Man who is at its centre is taken to be '*the* classical instance'. Here is a decisive and distinctive disclosure and release of God's *chesed*, which has been received, responded to and followed in a similarly decisive and distinctive fashion.

As a part of the event, then, the mother of Jesus is one of the factors which contributes mightily to the resultant picture of God. Of course she is not taken to be 'divine'; she is genuinely human, as was her son. But the portrayal of 'the Mother and Child' in Christian art does not mislead us. Here we see Jesus with Mary his mother. He was first a baby in her arms. Then as Christian thought about her developed, we have a portrayal of Mary as one who is understood to be herself caught up into the impact which the originative event has made upon those who have known it and responded to it. In those groups of Christian believers which have neglected her there has often been a far too aggressively 'masculine' portrayal of God; while in those parts of the tradition where she has been given a significant role the portrayal of God includes and stresses the stereotypically 'feminine', for the concept of God has been qualified by what is said about Jesus' mother and her love for her son.

In the christological development up to and through the Council of Chalcedon, a specific term was often used to describe Mary, and has been retained in much subsequent teaching. She was called *theotokos*, 'bearer of God'. Sometimes, indeed frequently, this word has been incorrectly translated as 'mother of God'. The Antiochene theologians, however, rejected that particular term, although Nestorius (in *The Bazaar of Hereacleides*, a work discovered and made available in our century and containing his reflections on the long controversy between Alexandrians and Antiochenes) finally could allow *theotokos* to be used as a possible term although it was one which he disliked because it was misleading. Instead of that term, he and the other Antiochenes preferred *christotokos*, 'the bearer' (or 'mother') of that One who has become known as 'the Christ' – which is to say, the supreme human instrument or agent for the divine word or divine 'Self-Expression' *vis-à-vis* humankind.

How could one talk meaningfully about 'mother of God', or even 'bearer of God'? To the Antiochenes it savoured of paganism; and to some of us today it is simply absurd to speak of God's having a mother. In the christological discussion of the time and the later discussion, this objection was met by a doctrine that so emphasized the divine in the reality of Jesus that his humanity was given a very secondary place. The 'self' of Jesus was said to be divine and not human and the device for making such teaching plausible was saying that Jesus' manhood was *enhypostatic* – its true centre was in the *Logos* or divine Word. To speak that way might perhaps have been acceptable, if due attention was paid to the fullness of his humanity. But unfortunately, what in fact has happened is that the *enhypostasia* has very often been understood as *anhypostasia* (or 'without human selfhood') and this has meant in practice that the full reality of his humanity has either been denied or seriously reduced so that it becomes much less than a genuine reality in his life.

In the course of this book I have consistently written of Mary as the mother of Jesus, never as 'the mother of God'. I could just as well have written that she was the mother of the humanity of the One who is accepted as 'the Christ' – thus she could be called (with the Antiochenes) *christotokos*.

For Christian faith this requires that in Jesus there is an action of God through an 'elected' Man, which the Jewish term Messiah originally intended. Now we must ask when that 'election' of the Man took place.

The theological function of the stories in Matthew and Luke about the 'virginal conception' of Jesus is to answer that question and to affirm that Jesus as the Christ is not to be taken as an after-thought on God's part in the divine-human relationship. Sometimes the same idea is expressed, as in John's Gospel, in parts of the Pauline literature, and in the tractate known as the epistle to the Hebrews, by reference to a 'pre-existence' to the happenings in nature and history. But nobody ought to assume that for classical theology Jesus as *that particular Man* 'pre-existed'. Responsible theologians have never made any such assertion, although in a good deal of popular piety, there has been a tendency in that direction, found not least in some of the more exuberant hymnody of the church.

But to the semitic mind talk about 'pre-existence' was a way of declaring the supreme importance or abiding value of events manifesting the divine providence in and governance of things. Similarly we find in Islam a concept of the Koran as 'pre-existent' to its writing down by Muhammad. Indeed, sometimes in Islamic talk there is even a strange reference to God spending eternity 'studying the Koran'!! 'Pre-existence' is for semitic thought a mythological way of asserting the abiding reality of the subject in question. To take it literally is to fall victim to theological absurdity. But to fail to take it seriously and to neglect what it is seeking to declare is to lessen the 'abiding reality' of that which is under discussion. Thus the so-called 'virgin birth' material in the New Testament is one way – not the only one, to be sure, for (as we have seen) the Johannine writer has another – of giving genuine content, doubtless often expressed in pious legend or Jewish *haggadah*, to the continuing insight of Christian faith that this Jesus, as the centre of the event called by his name, is of inescapable and enduring significance. In the Whiteheadian idiom that I have frequently used in this book, that event is important in the highest degree. And what has been accomplished by God in and through it is a focal and decisive clue to the divine character and the divine activity in the world.

Granted all this, and in view of the remarks made earlier about the problems associated with the use of *theotokos* ('the bearer of God' or 'mother of God'), I confess that I find that only that one phrase in the lovely devotion to St Mary called 'the Hail Mary' presents a difficulty.

'Hail Mary, full of grace. The Lord is with thee. Blessed art thou among women and blessed is the fruit of thy womb, Jesus. Holy Mary, *Mother of God*, pray for us sinners now and at the hour of our death.' Bishop Charles Gore once remarked (to someone who objected that this devotion seemed to approach paganism): 'On the contrary, it approaches St Luke's words in his Gospel.' That certainly is the case with the first phrases. The latter part of this traditional devotion has to do with the response of Christian faith to Mary's role in respect of her son; it is of course tied in with the teaching about intercession which is part of the wider Catholic belief in the 'communion of saints'. For anyone who is prepared to allow such intercession the second part of the devotion is then perfectly licit – save for the italicized phrase 'Mother of God'. I have indicated my objection to it on christological grounds. But if we alter that phrase to read 'mother of our Lord' or 'mother of Jesus Christ' or something similar, the petition is unobjectionable. In any event, what are the 'saints' doing in 'heaven' if they are not engaging in ceaseless prayer?

I do not propose to discuss here the basic issue of what that 'being in heaven' may signify; in the final chapter of this book something will be said about it. But I do wish at this point to insist that praying, wherever and whenever engaged in by persons in any culture or tradition, is an inescapable human practice. One recalls the words of Alfred Lord Tennyson in *The Idylls of the King*, where he speaks of such prayer, for which his hero King Arthur has asked, as so important that by it

> ' ... the whole round world is every way
> Bound by gold chains about the feet of God.'

In whatever fashion we may wish to understand the prayers of 'the blessed in heaven' who have been received into the divine life and who are unfailingly remembered in that life for what they were and for what they have done, surely God as the Love which is both paternal and maternal must value such praying.

Not only in Christian faith itself but also in the wider conceptuality which I am using in this book as a context for that faith God is both active and passive. Not only is God effectual in the created world; God is also affected by that creation. There is a give-and-take, a mutuality which has not always been given its due place in theological discussion. All too often in that discussion God is denied any affect from what the creation does, in its work or in its worship. It is assumed that the creation has a genuine relationship with God because it depends upon divine creative activity; but God is thought to have no real (only a 'logical') relationship with the world. This view makes the world irrelevant to the divine reality, since that divine reality could, so to say, 'get along' very nicely without 'a' world – not just the one we know but any conceivable creation. This seems to me to be linguistic nonsense. To speak of a creator without a creation makes no sense at all. Obviously we have here broached a subject not directly related to the main theme of our discussion, yet with its own importance for that theme.

But to return to our main theme point. I urge that Mary is indeed so much a part of the total Christian event both in its originative moment and in its continuation in history, that the event is improperly interpreted when she is left out of it. A 'chastened' devotion to St Mary, with a veneration which is never confused with the *latreia* or divine worship properly addressed to God alone, is invaluable. This is particularly significant because the act of God in Jesus Christ requires a human response such as that which was initially given in Mary's consent to the divine purpose; and when she is thus given a place in the total event, the spirituality which results is greatly enriched by the presence in it of what we mean when we speak of 'the feminine'. And in our own day, with an anti-macho revolt by many women and a reaction by the rest of us against the conventional far too 'male' portrayal of God, this is of inestimable value.

Some final comments may be made in this connection. One has to do with the need for a much more adequate awareness of the role and place of the feminine in the life of the Christian community. In principle this role and place has always been granted. Yet it needs implementation in many ways, one of which is the admittance of women (without hesitation) to the ordained ministry of the church. Another is the use in the church of language which is not 'sexist' but which accepts the feminine in its picture of God and of God's workings in the human and natural realms.

Still another comment is that what is crucial here is not devotion or spirituality alone, and not only ecclesiastical 'holy orders', but a profound theological awareness of that feminine aspect of creation. When the female sex, of whom Mary is a symbol and representative, is thus honoured something happens. If all humankind has its own dignity, responsibility and worth in the sight of God – the God who respects and employs them, with divine action 'conditioned' by the responsive co-operation of the men and women whom God loves – if this be the case, then we cannot evade giving to women their rightful place in all human affairs generally as well as in the Christian community in particular. The Pauline view that man is 'the head of woman' can no longer be accepted. It was a part of the apostle's inevitable sharing in ideas which he had received from the Jewish tradition. But even in Judaism we see today that women are claiming, and now and again receiving, their due recognition (and in a few instances are being admitted to the rabbinate).

In the early days of the church certain terms were used which have been seriously misinterpreted by those who (primarily, I think, for 'non-theological' reasons) refuse to grant to the female sex its proper place in the whole economy of God. The ancient fathers of the church had no thought of such a position for women as I have here advocated but they did use certain Greek and Latin words which are worth our attention. They did *not* say (in the Greek tongue) that in Jesus Christ God 'took' (as they would phrase it) masculine humanity or *andros*, but rather that God took *anthropos* (humankind in general or in their idiom 'manhood', *not* 'maleness'). They did *not* speak (in the Latin tongue) of God's 'assuming' (again to use their way of putting it) *vir* or masculine humanity but rather *homo* or humanity ('manhood') in general. If God did 'take' or 'assume' manhood or humankind, of course God did it in specific instances, appropriate to the given time and place when he did this. In terms of contemporary Jewish thought and practice, we should expect that this would be in masculine ways since women were not then accorded the recognition that was given to males.

Yet my main point remains valid. What we need here is Bishop Westcott's conception of a 'proportional' interpretation of biblical material – and patriotic material, too. Or in the words of Leonard Hodgson, my old teacher whom I delight to quote, 'What must be the truth for us if people who thought like that said what they did say?'

There are quite practical values at stake here; and with them we shall concern ourselves in the next chapter.

7

Practical Values

I remember, as if it were yesterday, a remark made in 1934, in his lecture on christology at the General Theological Seminary, by my beloved teacher who was later to be my equally beloved colleague, Marshall Bowyer Stewart. This is what he said to some forty young ordinands: 'When you get into a parish you will find in the church lots of stained glass windows with representations of Jesus. There will be Jesus on the cross, Jesus "risen from the dead", Jesus the preacher of the Sermon on the Mount. But unless somewhere in that church there is also some portrayal of Jesus as a baby in his mother's arms, you won't have the whole thing; you won't have the full picture of Jesus.'

Dr Stewart might have added further references such as, Jesus on the cross with Mary present with him, Jesus at the marriage feast at Cana with his mother among the guests. Jesus with John and Mary at the crucifixion, Jesus held by his mother when he was taken down from the cross (as represented for example in Michelangelo's *Pietà* in St Peter's in Rome), and of course the annunciation when Mary heard 'the message of the angel'. He might have made reference to the account in Acts of gatherings of the first Christian believers after the resurrection with Mary among them.

But not only are there these artistic portrayals. There is also much in literature which would be equally significant. I think here of two representative instances which can stand for countless others: Whitehead's words about the 'essence' of Christianity, in which he spoke of 'the mother, the child and the bare manger'; and Alice Meynell's poem 'Christ in the Universe' with its reference to 'the message to the Maid, the human lessons and the Young Man crucified'.

All this is an indication of what I have called the part which the mother of Jesus has come to have in the total event of Jesus Christ. And it suggests again the emphasis with which I ended the last chapter. Somehow or other a woman, a member of the female sex, must be seen as having a significant role in the disclosure and release of God as Love, enacted in the event of Jesus Christ in its wholeness.

One of the practical values of mariological devotion is precisely here. If we are to have a full and adequate understanding of God's loving action for humankind, we must have due recognition of the plain fact that the female, quite as much as the male, has its inescapable place in our thinking. To see this clearly and to use it faithfully in our spiritual as well as in our theological concerns, valuing both the historical material and also the mythological way in which it is expressed will bring an enriched response to the divine activity in human existence. The statements about such worth made by those who speak for the feminist movement today are more than understandable; they are an invaluable affirmation of the female component in the Christian story. The living tradition in its main-stream through Catholic piety and Catholic thought has always understood this, even if it has not properly implemented its understanding. Those who have failed in this understanding or its implementation have been responsible, albeit usually quite unintentionally, for a sad impoverishment of Christian faith and worship and life. They have been too narrowly intellectual, too exclusively moralistic, too intensely 'male' in their thinking. They have neglected something that makes for the warmth and graciousness of the total Christian life.

I want to stress once again the way in which the living tradition in its Catholic strain has been able – doubtless often with exaggeration and imbalance – to bring to Christians what I have just called warmth and graciousness. And I might again add here, to bring a wonderful tenderness as well. Bare churches, didactic preaching and teaching, portrayal of deity in an almost aggressive, dictatorial, and indeed often tyrannical fashion, relieved only by the one art which has received approval – that is, music in its various forms – have deprived God's children of much that makes life lovely and enriching.

In association with this practical value found in mariological practice and thought, we may mention two other significant points. In the figure of Mary, it is often said, there are combined two aspects of femininity which have meant most in human life: chastity and motherhood. Concentration on these would be wrong if other points were forgotten or minimized. Nevertheless there can be no doubt that these two have been significant in human experience. The concern for chastity taken alone has sometimes been focussed on what seems to be nothing other than attempted sexlessness; and hence the story of the virginal conception has become a way of denigrating sexuality in human existence. But that need not be done. It would be wiser if we defined chastity in the fashion urged by John Macmurray in several of his books, and saw that true chastity is not the denial or rejection of human sexual expression but, rather, is what he called 'emotional sincerity'. A chaste person is one who in his or her behaviour manifests a sincerity – a 'purity of heart' in the phrase from the Beatitudes, which Kierkegaard so well described as 'willing one thing' – which is neither cold nor remote but which involves the dedicated emotional life of the whole person. And maternity – the mother with her child – need not exclude that sort of chastity. Indeed, it goes along with it, for what nowadays is somewhat cynically called 'tender loving care' on the part of the maternal parent is also a 'willing one thing', with an emotional intensity which makes the representations of maternity so lovely and compelling in portraiture, sculpture and writing.

There can be danger here if this chastity and maternal love, and indeed if love itself, should be regarded as merely sentimental; the resultant picture is then a denial of the presence of anguish in human life. But genuine love (maternal or other) is surely not the negation of anguish; on the contrary, any love which has depth is a love that has experienced and known precisely such anguish. I like to quote the Spanish peasant who said that 'making love is declaring one's sadness'. Exaggerated as this may seem, it indicates something that all human lovers have experienced. And we may remember that in the Lukan story which tells of Simeon's blessing of Jesus and Mary on their visit to the temple, the old man is made to say to Mary that 'a sword shall pierce through thy own soul' (Luke 2.35). Doubtless this story is part of the haggadic material written up by the evangelist from some bits of early tradition about the birth of Jesus. Yet it speaks of what must indeed have been the experience of Jesus' mother, not only in the days of her son's infancy but also as she followed his career and above all as she witnessed his agony on the cross.

In one of the churches in Rome there is a famous piece of sculpture by Bernini which shows St Theresa of Avila pierced by a sword held by one of the seraphim. I have always felt that sculpture to be very moving, although I know that some have thought it to be too explicitly 'sexual in its suggestion'. But what does it matter if it is indeed in some real sense thus 'sexual in suggestion'? Perhaps that makes it the more compelling, because sexual experience, when it is most profound and all-embracing, is not simply sweet and painless. Far from it. It is likely to include precisely such anguish or pain or 'piercing of the soul' as that about which we have been speaking. Furthermore we may remember that real compassion – as the word itself tells us when we consider its derivation from Latin 'suffering with', or *cum* plus *patior* – is no superficial and cheerful observation of the pain of others. On the contrary, it is a sharing in that pain, a genuine experience of the anguish which is central in the deepest moments of our human loving.

In such an interpretation we are led to see, by the plain fact that Mary has her part in the total event of Christ – although of course not so obviously as by the suffering of her son 'for us and for our salvation' – that between God and God's children there is fellow feeling or compassion of the most exacting and awe-ful sort. No matter what theologians may have said, deep Christian devotion has never been prepared to think of God as 'impassable' or unable to experience suffering. As we have seen earlier, in the relationship which exists between God and the world, with humanity in its sorrows quite as much as in its delights, God must be understood as affected by what has happened to and in that creation. Thus we may see a practical religious value in the mariological aspect of Christian spirituality, precisely in the recognition of the reality of suffering in God, who is indeed a sharer with us of all that is felt deeply in the course of human existence.

If Mary stands for the chastity which is 'emotional sincerity' and for the wonder and pain of maternal love, she also has her place in what traditional piety has often called the 'Holy Family'. Familial life, which of course must also include the role of Joseph as a caring father, is hallowed and given heightened significance when we look at the frequent artistic portrayals of Mary and Joseph and Jesus together in the home at Nazareth. Refusal by Christians to contemplate this familial unity has produced still another kind of aridity or barrenness in their spirituality. Readiness to see and reverence the 'Holy Family', on the other hand, has led to a deep awareness of the blessedness of family life, where parents (and especially the mother) with their children are taken to represent an invaluable part of human life blessed and empowered by God.

Unquestionably stress on this sort of material, and taking about it the kind of position which I have been urging in this chapter, is not verifiable historically if we attend only to what used to be known as 'the assured results of biblical criticism'. Of course I must frankly admit this. But I would add (and indeed I would insist) that much in the developing mythology about Mary (and of course about the 'Holy Family' as well) need not be dismissed as so much fancy. I should wish to claim that such mythological discourse has been getting at something that is both significant and valuable. It is significant because it relates Mary to the whole picture of the event of Jesus Christ; it is valuable because it expresses a 'way' of Christian spiritual understanding and inspires concrete devotional attitudes and acts which have produced – or so at least many of us would say – a rich and enhancing kind of discipleship.

Much the same may be said about the practical value which is found in the thought of Mary's receptivity and responsiveness to God's calling. Here we come again to the way in which she has been seen as the 'consenting' human cause of the act of God in Christ, or to use traditional language, 'the incarnation' with its corollary in 'the atonement', redemption wrought by the act of God in humankind. As the model for Christian discipleship, the figure of Mary awakens and nourishes in others a similar receptivity to the divine movement in and upon human life with a similar responsiveness to whatever is taken to be the vocation or calling proper to each and every one of us.

Along with this there are the faithfulness, hopefulness or 'expectancy' of God's accomplishing the divine aim or purpose, and the lovingness, about which we spoke in an earlier chapter. In the traditional portrayal of Jesus' mother they are seen to be acted out in the concrete affairs of humanity. The 'model' awakens in the rest of us a desire to show similar faithfulness to God, expectancy of the divine action in us and in the world, and deep love in a ready obedience. Mary's example of dedication or commitment to the 'Love that moves the sun and the other stars', in Dante's splendid phrase at the end of *The Divine Comedy*, can awaken in Christian disciples their own readiness to allow that Love to move us. For the strongest power in the world is the divine Love; and to say 'Yes' to that divine Love and to endeavour to live in loving response to God's continuing invitation and lure, is to approach more and more nearly to our God-given vocation to become true sons and daughters of God.

There is yet another way in which we may benefit from a devout attention to Mary. It is suggested by some words from Mother Julian of Norwich, that remarkable great Anglican saint. In one of her 'shewings', she tells us she saw 'our Lady Saint Mary'; and she writes in this way about her vision: 'Our Lord showed me our Lady Saint Mary to teach us this: that it was the wisdom and truth in her, when she beheld her Maker, that enabled her to know him as so great, so holy, so mighty and so good. His greatness and his nobleness overwhelmed her. She saw herself as so little and low, so simple and poor, compared with God, that she was filled with humility. And so from this humble state she was lifted up to grace and filled with all manner of virtue and stands above all.' Thus Mother Julian sees the humility of the mother of Jesus and God's rewarding this humility.

We may recall here the words of the *Magnificat* put into Mary's mouth in Luke's Gospel (2.46ff.). They are familiar words for those who attend Evensong in Anglican cathedrals and in other churches where they are said or sung each day: 'My soul doth magnify the Lord; and my spirit hath rejoiced in God my Saviour.' Notice how Julian's account of Mary's humility is given supreme expression in that Lukan 'Song of Mary': 'He hath regarded the low estate of his handmaiden; for behold, from henceforth all generations shall call me blessed. For he that is mighty has done great things; and holy is his name. And his mercy is on them that fear him, throughout all generations. He hath shewed strength with his arm; he hath scattered the proud in the imagination of their hearts. He hath put down the mighty from their seats and hath exalted the humble and meek. He hath filled the hungry with good things; and the rich he hath sent empty away...'

Humility, on the one hand; exaltation in consequence of such humility, on the other: how remarkably these are linked together in Mary's song! God's strength is shown to those who are humble in the divine presence; while the proud, the arrogant, the assertive and the aggressive are 'put down from their seats'. God 'regards the low estate of his handmaiden'; and it is because of Mary's 'lowliness' that she is to be called from henceforth, by all generations, 'the one who is blessed'.

How are we to understand such humility and how express it in our Christian discipleship? First of all, of course, we must see that genuine humility is not cringing nor servile submission to a coercive force exercised upon us. Rather, it is the ready acceptance of the divine purpose for us. It is not a matter of becoming a Uriah Heep, as portrayed in Charles Dickens' novel: one who invites others to see him as a door-mat and to walk over him. In contrast to that, perhaps I may suggest that humility, from one point of view, is identical with a sense of humour! The person who has a sense of humour at its best is one who makes no proud claims, who does not pretend to be other than he or she really is, and who recognizes that it is equally absurd to talk and think all the time about oneself. Humility is a way of being aware of the truth about ourselves. Above all it is to grasp the humbling truth that only God is great.

At the same time, creaturely humility is a reflection of an even more devastating truth: that God is humble. To say this may seem shocking to some people. After all, they will point out, you have just said that God is 'great'. Yes; but the divine greatness, once there is serious Christian awareness of the disclosure of divinity in the event of Jesus Christ, is not to be seen as a matter of God's vaunting or boasting of self or of God's 'lording' it over the creatures. The divine greatness is very different from our usual human ideas of greatness. It is a greatness which shows itself in self-giving, in ceaseless caring, in constant concern and in a readiness to come to the help of others in their need. In this sense, the *Magnificat* is a revolutionary song. It turns our human pretensions upside down and it shows us the God who is on the side of those who are oppressed, not on the side of those who 'exalt themselves'. This same insight of course was present in a good deal of Jewish prophetic witness. But it receives vivid and compelling statement in its manifestation in Mary. It has there 'a local habitation and a name'.

Most of us regard highly self-assertive or overly proud men and women as unhappy specimens of humanity. Such people seem to us to be more than just mistaken in their self-exaltation; they are ridiculous in their pretensions. We are inclined to say that 'They will get their come-uppance' and when they do, we shall have a sneaking pleasure in their downfall! Of course that is wrong on our part. If we were like Jesus, who (we are told in John's Gospel) 'knew what was in humankind', we might be more charitable in our judgment, because in a strange way people like that are probably not fully aware of what they are like; they are blinded by their own conviction of status or position or privilege. It is more a tragic than a laughable matter that they are as they are and that inevitably they will tumble down from their position of supposed superiority. Deep down in our human existence, we know that an unaffected humility is the only way in which we can come to terms with ourselves and with our actual place in the scheme of things; and perhaps we need to sympathize with the unfortunate people who do not recognize this.

Mother Julian's insistence that 'the creature' must always be 'marvellously meek and mild' finds its vivid illustration in Mary. But meekness and mildness are not to be taken as negative passivity. In the Christian way of seeing things they are instances of what may be called an 'active passivity' whose corollary is a 'passive activity'. To be acted upon by God, and to be ready for and accepting of this, is Mary's virtue as the tradition has understood it and as the material in Luke shows it.

That passivity is indeed active, as I have just said; it leads to the doing of what we are given by God to do. Surely in our experience those who are open to the impact of others are also those most likely to act positively for the other's benefit. And in God, a Christian may dare to claim, something of the same sort is to be seen. God can be acted upon and God is acted upon. God is genuinely influenced and affected by what goes on in the world; and God then re-acts, as we might put it, by making the divine love still more available to the creatures.

One of the ways in which the Process conceptuality which has been used in this book can help us is precisely here. When that conceptuality is taken up and employed by Christian thinkers the bold claim may be made that God *is* like that: passive *and* active – as we have seen. Much theologizing has thought to exalt deity by saying exactly the opposite. It has been assumed that God's creation can do nothing for God; God is in charge and our duty is to bow before the divine presence, not with such genuine humility as I have been urging but with a kind of servility appropriate only to essentially worthless creatures – a 'vermiform' or wormlike understanding of humanity. I wish to urge the contrary view: that God wants, and in at least one sense needs, creaturely – and human – response to the divine purpose of amorization with its correlative in justice and truth and beauty. God is humble; the divine humility is precisely in this readiness to be acted upon. An old friend once put it well: 'God does not obtrude or intrude, neither does God make coercive demands. What God does is just to act initially in love and invitation and then to act responsively in persuasion and further invitation.'

Furthermore, the divine love is strangely promiscuous. God is concerned for all, not just for a select few. But even in the divine 'election', for special purposes – as some theologians would phrase it – God does not over-ride human consent. He invites it. Hence the stress in this book on 'consent' from the creatures. Karl Barth, the great Swiss theologian of the generation just past, was accustomed to argue that while Jesus Christ is certainly 'the Elect Man' – since in the event of Christ God has chosen to act in a focal and decisive fashion, so far as we who are Christian can understand it – God also 'elects' all humankind to be 'in the Son'. Thus this Son is indeed 'the first born of many brethren'. Unlike the strict Calvinist idea that 'election' is highly selective and functions in what seems an arbitrary fashion, Barth's teaching gives it a universalist quality. And whatever else in Barthian theology may be thought unfortunate, here at least is a point which is profoundly 'evangelical': it is tied in with a sure grasp of the gospel in which the divine Love is accorded supreme place.

I conclude this chapter with a final emphasis. In the totality of human experience, and not just in the specifically Christian event and its 'stream of influence', we should be prepared to see the divine activity in love. Among other things this will mean that Christian 'imperialism' (as Arnold Toynbee once called it) will be impossible. In most diverse ways in the non-Christian religions, each appropriate to a different culture, God is active. God is never 'left without witness' in the human heart. In many of these religions there is an intimation, sometimes even more than an intimation, of what has been urged in this chapter. Above all the role of the feminine in religious understanding and life is often to be found in these religions. In that case, non-Christian ways in which the divine reality has been seen often enough as much more on the feminine than on the masculine side are of inestimable value. And we should be ready to confess that a good deal of Western Christian culture in its religious expression has been sadly deficient in this very respect.

If something like this can be said, we may conclude that the place given to Mary in the living tradition of Christianity, chiefly in its Eastern Orthodox and Catholic expression, is by no means accidental. Nobody within that tradition would wish to say that Mary herself is divine. But she can properly be seen as part of the event of Jesus Christ and hence integral to the total fact of Christ in all its complexity and its unity. What I have been calling the 'practical value' of mariological interest and concern, as well as the 'chastened' devotion of veneration accorded her, is not to be taken as the expression of some supposedly 'Catholic prejudice' but rather to be seen as somehow at the heart of the Christian reality. Once more, then, we can make our own the traditional words from the 'Hail Mary': 'Blessed art thou among women.' And we can do this because first of all we have been brought to say of her, 'Blessed is the fruit of thy womb, Jesus.'

8

Mary and Christian Faith Today

Much of what has been said in this book may be rejected altogether by some Christians; or it may be taken as a nostalgic attempt on my part to preserve a type of spirituality for which there is no sound historical or theological basis. Extreme Protestant Christians will very likely say that any talk about mariological devotion is in effect an argument for the paganism which threatens what in Scotland are so splendidly called 'the crown rights of Jesus Christ'. More liberal-minded Protestants may think that because we know so little about the historical figure of Mary, we should disregard the whole business; in any event, they may ask, what is the point of stressing the mythological nature of much of the given material when one follows this by urging that the subject of that material is worthy of a genuine veneration? Conservative Roman Catholics are certain to say that the whole approach cuts at the roots of the devotion that we should given to Mary in our Christian life. And many of those who follow the Process conceptuality which for years I have adopted as helpful for us in our effort to give a proper context for Christian faith are likely to dismiss the whole enterprise as misguided if not positively erroneous.

Nonetheless, I am still prepared to claim that there is genuine value and importance in the age-long attitude found in the Catholic tradition which permits and indeed encourages us to make our own the salutation which Luke's Gospel puts in the mouth of the angel at the annunciation: 'Hail Mary, divinely favoured! The Lord is with you. Blessed you are among women and blessed is the fruit of [your] womb.' I believe and have urged earlier that we may even take upon our lips the close of that traditional salutation as it has been made into a familiar prayer in the Western Catholic Church: 'Pray for us sinners, now and in the hour of our death' – although (as I have said) to call Mary 'Mother of God' certainly raises a difficult christological problem to which I gave attention in chapter 6. To speak of her as 'mother of Jesus' or 'mother of Christ' is entirely appropriate and I myself make that substitution in the use of the salutation.

Here then are some concluding remarks on the subject of mariological devotion.

First of all, I must dissociate myself from those who simply dismiss all mythological material as irrelevant. Of course it must be granted that historical data about Mary are very few and that a good deal of what purports to be history belongs rather in the category of legendary discourse. It is also true, as I have insisted, that whatever we do possess which is grounded in some veridical historical incident is communicated to us through the apostolic witness, whose major concern was not to give historical information about some supposed occurrences in the past but rather was to speak 'from faith to faith' – to proclaim the event in which Jesus is central and to awaken a response to him as One in whom there is a decisive action of God in, for, and with genuine human existence.

To recognize this about our material introduces us at once to the more general problem of the use of myth in religious discourse. But surely only in what might be styled mythological language – or, if you prefer, in the idiom of poetry of a highly imaginative sort – can we speak at all of

God's 'visiting and redeeming his people' or of 'a coming down' of God into the human realm, or of 'the Word made flesh'. This is not the language of ordinary literal predication – if indeed in any really important aspect of human experience literal predication is a possibility! In the deeply significant aspects or moments of that experience, we must necessarily talk in a non-literal fashion. For we are not dealing with subjects like mathematics or scientific observation or newspaper reporting. We are seeking to convey meanings which escape any such precision and which can only be spoken allusively and imaginatively. Hence I cannot think of mythological talk about Mary as nonsense. On the contrary, I believe that it may very well point to truth which is highly relevant to us humans and which in the realm of Christian faith cannot be dismissed out of hand.

Secondly, there can be no doubt that in the age-long central Christian tradition the figure of Mary has always had its honoured place. That place given her in the tradition in no way minimizes, and certainly does not deny, the centrality of her Son in the picture. His 'crown rights' are never called in question. And precisely because in that tradition she is the mother of Jesus, the supreme place and role of Jesus himself is emphasized. It is as the 'bearer' of that same Jesus, and only in that context, that she is spoken about at all.

Furthermore, if there is validity in the thought that in some real sense Mary was the 'consenting cause' of what God has done in the event of which Jesus is centre, her role becomes the more significant. This might be phrased in the fashion in which I recently heard a preacher put it: 'If every son and daughter of the human race is largely "formed" by parental influence, above all by the influence of his or her mother, St Mary is surely an important figure in Christian thought.' We need not insist on a vividly conscious response on Mary's part to the vocation which was hers in becoming the mother of her son; indeed, to think that there was such a vivid conscious awareness is to think the incredible. Yet through her care and love for her son, in her own concern and devotion, she must in a real fashion have been formative in the development of that son's sense of vocation and in his readiness to obey what he took to be the divine purpose for his life.

I have sketched earlier what seem to me to be important theological points relevant to our understanding of the divine character and to our conception of how God acts in the realm of creaturely affairs. For a Christian Process thinker, the central point here has to do with God's innermost quality and God's outward-going movement as persuasive and loving, rather than as coercive. God works upon, in, and with the creatures; God waits upon their response and does not force himself or herself on the creation. That is the controlling fact – and it is one which much classical theism does not seem able to comprehend. But the Process conceptuality, or what Charles Hartshorne has called 'neo-classical theism', is ready to accept this and to insist upon it. The created order has its influence and affect upon God; it is really, not simply (as in classical theism) logically, related to deity.

A good deal of conventional Reformed theology from its earliest days – and I have phrased it in this way because Lutheranism seems often to have been a remarkable exception – has been too masculine in its portrayal of God. Of course, what has been lacking in it has been the value of the feminine in human experience. I do not suggest that Mary is to be made 'part of the Godhead'! What I do insist is that total rejection of Mary as integrally part of the event of Jesus Christ is all too likely to produce exactly that excessively male image of God; whereas the tradition in which she has been given a feminine place has been much more ready to allow for, even to stress, what is stereotypically feminine: receptivity, deep emotional response, gentleness and participation. Perhaps one significant aspect of Mary's place in the total event of Jesus Christ is to bring vividly before us precisely that fuller interpretation of the divine love.

Here again we have to do with what earlier I called 'active passivity and passive activity' in the divine ways of working. In our Christian understanding it seems essential that the most certain way to achieve God-intended results in the over-all God-world relationship is through the kind of activity which is patient and ready in accepting from others; while on the other hand, the kind of passivity which is not non-action (and hence inert and static) but a zealous 'waiting upon' response, is likely to achieve more than coercive pressure which often arouses refusal or rejection on the part of the victim of such pressure.

The largely mythological portrayal of Mary brings to the fore what I have styled the elements most central to genuine Christian discipleship. Mary is pictured as obedient to God's call, as faithful in her response, as caring and loving towards her child, as loyal to him in moments when she did not understand what he was doing. She is pictured with him at his crucifixion and sharing in the company of his followers after his death. She is mentioned as one of the post-resurrection group of believers. Doubtless she did not understand all that was going on; so the stories themselves tell us. Yet she is always portrayed as the loving mother whose care was not refused when (so to say) 'things were going badly for her son'. She 'hung on' 'through thick and thin'. I have said in all this that she is indeed an appropriate symbolic expression of what true Christian discipleship must be like. And the same may be said of her as 'the type' of the church and of the creation when it is on the right path and hence (as the tradition says) 'redeemed' to serve God's abiding purpose of amorization.

I urge therefore that there can be nothing wrong about a

'chastened' variety of devotion to St Mary. There is no reason why we may not deeply respect the figure which the whole range of stories, some with historical basis and others more legendary, brings before us. If imaginative response is important in religious life, we have here a signal instance which can evoke that kind of response. What is more, there is here also a positive significance which cannot be denied. For when Mary has been called 'blessed among women' and has been accorded the veneration which that 'blessedness' receives, when she has been regarded – in the developed early myth – as the mother of all Christians and of the fellowship which constitutes the Christian church, a specific kind of religious life has emerged. Some may reject that kind of Christian life as soft or sentimental in one sense, altogether too 'passive' and lacking the positive quality of 'doing things'. The result then may be what I have described as an extreme sort of insistence on a masculine and aggressive picture of God who demands from the creatures a servile obedience to an imposed divine demand. Personally I find that portrayal of God highly offensive, not least because it turns God into an imperious dictator or tyrant, rather than a loving yet always adamant parent. In biblical idiom, we need to emphasize 'our heavenly father' rather than what some revised liturgies (in the *Sanctus* in the eucharist) have so unhappily named the 'God of power and might' – and have even done this with no insistence that God's 'power and might' are a reflection of the Love which in Wesley's words is 'his nature and his name'.

It has been said that Protestant religion 'brings men to their feet', whilst Catholic piety 'brings them to their knees'. The implication is that the latter is weak and ineffectual while the former is vigorous and effectual. I think that the saying is quite misleading. Why? Because worship in its true meaning, in which humans are indeed 'brought to their knees', is the necessary condition for activity if such activity

– on their feet! – is to be anything more than futile activism. George Tyrrell, tragic leader of Roman Catholic Modernism in the early part of this century, once said that 'There are some who think that Christianity is "going about doing good", more particularly the kind of "doing good" which involves a great deal of "going about".' That was an uncharitable and probably an unfair remark: yet it had a point. For the activism which characterizes much contemporary Christian behaviour reminds one of another biting remark, this time by George Santayana and about the 'fanatic who' (he said) 'redoubles his effort when he has forgotten his aim'.

The prior condition of significant and (in the long run) effectual activity is awareness of and dedication to the ends which are to be sought and served. In worship or prayer, 'on one's knees', we become aware of this necessity. In authentic Christianity this may be subsumed under the broad heading 'amorization', Teilhard de Chardin's word which I have already used. Christian spirituality or devotion is the necessary ground for Christian action, delivering that action from senseless striving. On the other hand, of course, prayer which does not lead to action of some sort is all too likely to be sterile.

It is in this general context that I should wish to defend what I have styled a 'chastened' devotion to the mother of the Lord. As the model for Christian discipleship, Mary can be taken to represent a kind of Christian dedication which is neither hectically active nor irrelevantly pious. It does not matter very much – in fact, I think that it hardly matters at all – that much of what we know about Mary is not susceptible of historical verification but is conveyed (and often through legendary tales) in a mythological fashion.

Much that has been said by pious people about Mary has been absurd, with nothing to commend it to us even if it has often been taken as part of official Roman Catholic and

Eastern Orthodox teaching. On the other hand, there is no reason to 'throw the baby out with the bath-water' by rejecting *in toto* the long tradition of veneration of and devotion to her. Why should we not be content with (and happy about) a 'chastened' reverence? And why should we not be prepared even to ask her prayers? If prayer matters, if God can and does use human response to the divine love in ways that may pass our understanding but yet be taken as appropriate in the God-human relationship, there seems no point in a refusal to say 'pray for us' when we venture to address the mother of Jesus.

In much traditional Eastern Orthodox practice, as I have noted, it is thought right to ask the prayers of all whom we have loved but who are now gone from this world and have somehow been received into the divine life and accepted by the God whose love is all-inclusive in scope but always particular in application. I cannot see why this is an unacceptable practice, unless we have subscribed to the view that death is the absolute end. But deep in Christian conviction is the affirmation that while death is indeed the ending of mortal existence for each of us, yet *in God* – the God who is for us our only genuine hope – all God's people are treasured, valued and remembered, in the ways that are possible for God but which we in our finitude cannot explain.

Whether or not there is a 'subjective immortality' for each one and hence a continuing conscious human awareness after death, the confidence remains that this same God responds to prayer in whatever way it is possible in divine loving concern for God to do. Can God not find point in our remembering the departed, for whom we dare to ask 'a place of light, refreshment and peace'? There is enduring validity in the notion that 'the prayers of a righteous person availeth much'. May there not be a divine response to a 'remembrance of Mary' such that we may ask her to pray for us? I believe there is; and I believe it because it is in accordance with what I take to be a truly Christian interpretation of how God and the whole created order are related.

Before I end this book, I wish to say that while from time to time, not only in this last chapter but also in earlier sections, I have spoken critically about much in conventional Protestant Christianity, this is very far from being my overall view of that kind of Christian belonging. There can be no doubt that the general Protestant or Reformed emphasis on the normative place of scripture as a 'testing ground' for the ongoing Christian tradition is both invaluable and necessary. Neither can there be any doubt that the Calvinistic stress on the divine sovereignty is of utmost importance, although one can wish that this had been presented more forcibly as the sovereignty of cosmic Love-in-act. Again, there is no question that the Lutheran insistence on 'justification by grace through faith only', taken up by other Reformers, is indeed (as Luther himself said) *articulus stantis aut cadentis ecclesiae*, 'the article of a standing or falling church'. It is a re-statement, in theological terms, of the New Testament conviction that nobody can 'earn' salvation by 'good works' but can receive it only through commitment in confident trust to God's gracious love as this is re-presented in the event of Jesus Christ. My intention here has been only to say that often, although not always, the spirituality which has been found in the Protestant tradition has lacked a specific quality present in the more Catholic tradition – a warmth and tenderness which I believe to be integral to the whole Christian enterprise.

Fortunately, one might say providentially, in contemporary Protestant circles, both as a matter of theology and in the liturgical expression of faith as well as in the understanding of the Christian life in grace, there has been a readiness to modify positions which (perhaps for historically explainable motives) marked the older variety of Protestantism. At the same time, in specifically Catholic circles the Reformed emphases noted in the last paragraph have been discovered or recovered. Hence we may very well be at the dawn of a new day, in which both kinds of Christian faith and discipleship will be drawn together, to influence one another in a fruitful fashion.

I think that this is to be welcomed with enthusiasm, not least because Anglicanism (my own stance, of course) has always sought to value both the traditional Catholic and the Reformed emphasis. I do not believe the Anglican communion has always been right! To say or think any such thing would be preposterous. Yet as a type of Christian witness which has valued and retained 'Catholic structures' but has also been open to much in the Protestant – Evangelical and Reformed – movements in Western Christianity, and which has enjoyed a sympathetic relationship with Eastern Orthodox Christianity, the Anglican communion has had its special significance. Although nowadays it seems somewhat trite to say it, it is true that Anglicanism has been a 'bridge' between more Catholic (and Orthodox) ways and more Protestant (or Evangelical and Reformed) ways. A bridge is intended to make it possible for those on either side of its span to communicate with each other. In that sense, and only in that sense, it is helpful to talk about an Anglican *via media* or 'middle path' which touches on both sides of Christian tradition.

When in the divine providence a full reunion of Christians comes about, the Anglican communion will probably lose its specific identity by its inclusion in what Canon Theodore Wedel once styled 'the coming great church'. For our present purpose, nevertheless, it is worth noting that Anglicans are in a good position to make a case for what I have ventured to describe figuratively as a 'chastened' mariological attitude and practice. The revival of mariological interest in the Anglican communion, owing so much to the Tractarian movement and its successor in Anglo-Catholicism, had its roots in Caroline piety in the seventeenth century. Hence it is a revival and not a complete novelty. Bishop Gore's observation that we owe to Mary 'all veneration short of worship' is an admirable statement with which we must agree. In many ways, to be sure, Bishop Gore was 'a defender of lost causes', as both Dean Inge and Professor Bethume-Baker used to say about him. His failure to develop his own theology along lines which he himself set forth in his famous christological essay in *Lux Mundi*, as well as his bitter persecution of some of the English Modernists in his later years, were lamentable and mistaken. Yet what he had to say about the place of the mother of Jesus and about the appropriate way of reverently regarding her still stands firm and sound. This book is an attempt to reinforce, in the light of a good deal of newer knowledge about the scriptures and the living Christian tradition, what Gore advocated and urged. If that is understood, then I am content.

But it is not only those of 'Anglican obedience' whom I have been addressing; it is also other Christians of good will who may be prepared at least to listen and who may find their own Christian faith, worship and life enriched greatly if they are brought to give to the mother of Jesus the honour which rightly belongs to her.

I quoted a few pages back from a sermon I heard recently on this subject. The preacher made the point to which I there referred, about how the mother of Jesus must have been such a one as to assist her son to fulfil his vocation. In the conclusion of his sermon this preacher went on to say that those who reverence Mary are by that very fact reverencing her son. It is to her son and to him alone that we who presume to call ourselves Christian owe our ultimate allegiance under God. In some fashion, explain it how we may, the son of Mary is for us both the focal disclosure of God and the decisive release of divine love into the world. To affirm this, and then to endeavour to live in terms of that affirmation, is the heart and centre of Christian faith. In that faith, I have argued, Mary has a very real although a subordinate role to play.

Appendix

Books by Norman Pittenger

1. *The Approach to Christianity*, Centenary Press, London 1939
2. American edition, *The Christian Way in a Modern World*, Cloister Press, Louisville, Kentucky, USA, 1944
3. Revised and enlarged British edition, *Principles and Practice of the Christian Faith*, SCM Press 1952
4. *This Holy Fellowship* (edited, with essay by N.P. and E.R. Hardy) Morehouse-Gorham Company, New York 1939
5. *Christ and Christian Faith*, Round Table Press, New York 1941
6. *Christian Belief and Practice*, Morehouse-Gorham Company, New York 1942
7. *Life of the Lord Jesus* (with B. I. Bell), St James's Publications, New York 1943
8. *As His Follower*, Episcopal Church Publications, New York 1943
9. *Stewards of the Mysteries of Christ*, Cloister Press, Louisville, Kentucky 1945
10. *His Body the Church*, Morehouse-Gorham Company, New York 1946
11. *The Divine Action*, Church Congress Publications, New York 1946
12. *A Living Faith for Living Men*, Cloister Press, Louisville, Kentucky 1946
13. *Sacraments, Signs, and Symbols*, Wilcox-Follett Company, Chicago 1949
14. *The College Militant* (with T.S.K. Scott-Craig), Guild of Scholars, New York 1949
15. *The Historic Faith in a Changing World*, Oxford University Press, New York 1950
16. *The Christian Sacrifice*, Oxford University Press, New York 1951
17. *The Faith of the Church* (with J.A. Pike), Seabury Press, New York 1950

18. *Our Faith and the Church* (with J.A. Pike) Seabury Press, New York 1953
19. *Christ in the Haunted Wood*, Seabury Press, New York 1953
20. *What is the Priesthood?* (with J. V. Butler), Morehouse-Gorham Company, New York 1954
21. *The Christian View of Sexual Behaviour*, Seabury Press, New York 1954
22. *Christian Affirmations*, Morehouse-Barlow Company, New York 1954
23. *Theology and Reality*, Seabury Press, New York 1956
24. *Rethinking the Christian Message*, Seabury Press, New York 1956
25. *Tomorrow's Faith Today*, Exposition Press, New York 1956
26. *The Church, the Ministry, and Reunion*, Seabury Press, New York 1957
27. *Unity in the Faith* (by W.P. Dubose, edited with essay by N.P.) Seabury Press, New York 1957
28. *The Episcopalian Way of Life*, Prentice-Hall, New York 1957
29. *The Word Incarnate*, Harper and Company, New York and Nisbet, London 1959
30. View Points (edited by N.P. and J.B. Cohurn) Seabury Press, New York 1959.
31. *The Pathway to Believing*, Bobbs-Merrill Company, Indianapolis 1960
32. *The Ministry of the Good Shepherd*, General Seminary Book Store, New York 1962
33. *Classics of the Middle Ages* (related and edited by N.P., translated into Chinese by F.P. Jones), Missionary Press, Hong Kong 1962
34. *Proclaiming Christ Today*, Seabury Press, New York and SPCK, London 1962
35. *The Christian Understanding of Human Nature*, Westminster Press, Philadelphia and Nisbet, London 1964
36. *Christian Prayer in a New Perspective*, Canterbury Fellowship of Australia, Melbourne, Australia 1966
37. *Love is the Clue*, Mowbrays, London and Forward Movement Publications, Cincinnati 1967
38. *Time for Consent*, SCM Press, London 1967; revised and enlarged editions 1976 and 1980
39. *God in Process*, SCM Press, London 1967
40. *The Life of Jesus Christ*, Franklin Watts Company, New York 1968

Appendix

41. *Reconceptions in Christian Thinking*, Seabury Press, New York 1968
42. *Life, Light, Love*, Mowbrays, London 1968
43. *The Life of St Paul*, Franklin Watts Company, New York 1968
44. *Process Thought and Christian Faith*, Nisbet, London and Macmillan, New York 1968
45. *Christ for us Today* (ed. by N.P.), SCM Press, London 1968
46. *Love Looks Deep*, Mowbrays, London 1969. USA edition under title of *The Only Meaning*, Forward Movement Publications, Cincinnati 1970
47. *Martin Luther*, Franklin Watts Company, New York 1969
48. *Alfred North Whitehead*, Lutterworth Press, London and John Knox Press, Richmond, Virginia 1969
49. *The Christian Situation*, Epworth Press, London 1969
50. *God's Way with Men*, Hodder and Stoughton, London and Judson Press, Valley Forge 1969
51. *Henry VIII*, Franklin Watts Company, New York 1970
52. *Richard the Lion-hearted*, Franklin Watts Company, New York 1970
53. *Christology Reconsidered*, SCM Press, London 1970
54. *Goodness Distorted*, Mowbrays, London 1970
55. *Pilgrim of Rome*, (ed. by N.P. [with essay] and C.D. Nelson), Nisbet, London 1970
56. *The Last Things in a Process Perspective*, Epworth Press, London 1970.
57. *Making Sexuality Human*, Pilgrim Press, Philadelphia 1970
58. *St Peter*, Franklin Watts Company, New York 1971
59. *Plato*, Franklin Watts Company, New York 1971
60. *The Christian Church as Social Process*, Epworth Press, London and Westminster Press, Philadephia 1971
61. *Early Britain*, Franklin Watts Company, New York 1972
62. *Life in Christ*, W.B. Eerdmanns Company, Grand Rapids, 1972
63. *Trying to be a Christian*, Pilgrim Press, Philadelphia 1972
64. *Life as Eucharist*, W.B. Eerdmanns Company, Grand Rapids 1973
65. *Christian Faith and the Question of History*, Fortress Press, Philadelphia 1973
66. *Love and Control in Human Sexuality*, Pilgrim Press, Philadelphia 1973
67. Praying Today, W.B. Eerdmanns Company, Grand Rapids 1974
68. *The Holy Spirit*, Pilgrim Press, New York 1974

69. *A Vision and a Way*, Forward Movement Publications, Cincinnati 1974

70. *Unbounded Love*, Seabury Press, New York 1976

71. *The Divine Triunity*, Pilgrim Press, New York 1977

72. *Gay Life-Styles*, Universal Fellowship Press, Los Angeles 1977

73. *Cosmic Love and Human Wrong*, Paulist Press, New York 1978

74. *Loving Says it All*, Pilgrim Press, New York 1978

75. *The Lure of Divine Love*, Pilgrim Press, New York and T.T. Clark, Edinburgh 1979

76. *Whither? The Shape of the Future* (ed. with essay, by N.P.) Modern Churchmen's Union, London 1979

77. *After Death: Life in God*, SCM Press, London and Seabury Press, New York 1980

78. *Astounding Grace*, Mowbrays, London 1981

79. *Catholic Faith in a Process Perspective*, Orbis Books, Maryknoll, NY 1981

80. *The Meaning of Being Human*, Pilgrim Press, New York 1982

81. *Picturing God*, SCM Press, London 1982

82. *The Ministry of All Christians*, Morehouse-Barlow Company, Wilton, Conn. 1983

83. *Preaching the Gospel*, Morehouse-Barlow Company, Wilton, Conn. 1984

84. *Passion and Perfection*, Forward Movement Publications, Cincinnati 1985

85. *Before the Ending of the Day*, Morehouse-Barlow Company, Wilton, Conn. 1985

86. *The Pilgrim Church and the Easter People*, Michael Glazier, Wilmington, Del. 1986.

87. *Freed to Love*, Morehouse-Barlow Company, Wilton, Conn. 1987

88. *Becoming and Belonging*, Morehouse Publishing, Wilton, Conn. 1989

89. *The Lord's Prayer*, Forward Movement Publications, Cincinnati 1989

90. *Our Lady: The Mother of Jesus in Christian Faith and Devotion*, SCM Press, London 1996

(The above list does not include all books edited by, or with essays written by, Norman Pittenger. A complete bibliography is deposited at the Library of the General Theological Seminary, New York City).